Little Laureates

East & West Sussex

Edited by Angela Fairbrace

YoungWriters
First published in Great Britain in 2007 by:
Young Writers
Remus House
Coltsfoot Drive
Peterborough
PE2 9JX
Telephone: 01733 890066
Website: www.youngwriters.co.uk

SB ISBN 978-1 84602 990 5

Foreword

Young Writers was established in 1991 and has been passionately devoted to the promotion of reading and writing in children and young adults ever since. The quest continues today. Young Writers remains as committed to the nurturing of poetic and literary talent as ever.

This year's Young Writers competition has proven as vibrant and dynamic as ever and we are delighted to present a showcase of the best poetry from across the UK and in some cases overseas. Each poem has been selected from a wealth of *Little Laureates* entries before ultimately being published in this, our sixteenth primary school poetry series.

Once again, we have been supremely impressed by the overall quality of the entries we have received. The imagination, energy and creativity which has gone into each young writer's entry made choosing the poems a challenging and often difficult but ultimately hugely rewarding task - the general high standard of the work submitted ensured this opportunity to bring their poetry to a larger appreciative audience.

We sincerely hope you are pleased with this final collection and that you will enjoy *Little Laureates East & West Sussex* for many years to come.

Contents

Ashurst CE (A) Primary School, Ashurst

Amelia Young (10)	1
Sam Wadman (10)	1
Lottie Arnold (10)	2
Charlotte Bridger (11)	3
Olivia Middleton (10)	4
Harry Fuggles (10)	5
Flori Pearcey (11)	6
Rebecca van Pelt (10)	7
Gabrielle Williams (9)	8
Joe Homshaw (11)	9
Charlie Nunn (10)	10
Douglas Ford (11)	10
Robert Loveless (9)	11

Bishop Tufnell Junior School, Bognor Regis

Danielle Golding (8)	11
Sophie Turner (9)	12
Danny Cooper (8)	12
Joshua Leslie (8)	12
Jessica Dawling (8)	13
Zak Boniface (9)	13
Ceara Rumsey (8)	13
Georgia Stevens (8)	14
Emma Last (8)	14
Julia McGee-Russell (9)	14
Elliot Playle-Howard (9)	15
Cameron Cousens (9)	15
Bradley Dodman (8)	15
Alana Kirkpatrick (8)	16
Jacob Lowery (8)	16
Bradley Atkins (8)	16
Daniel Cox (8)	17
Jade Longworth (8)	17
Demi Rishman (9)	17
Ashley Walpole (8)	18
Dean Edwards (9)	18
Samuel Baker (9)	18
Ross Edwards (8)	19

Beatrice Waters (9)	19
Kyra Beaven (8)	19
Eloise Kenchington (8)	20
Jack Hawkins (8)	20
Maisie Fleming (8)	20
Ezra Whitlock (8)	21
Paige Whiting (9)	21
Jacob White (9)	21
David Harris (8)	22
Kelsey Brooke (8)	22
Lilah Matthews (9)	22
Jade Fox (9)	23
Beth Clarke (9)	23
Dina Betsworth (8)	23
Giorgia Cappella (9)	24
Megan Lewis (8)	24
Ella Frye (8)	24
Joe Benjamin & Josh Clark (9)	25
Josh Markey (9) & Ross Stephenson-Gill (8)	25
Paige Knight (8)	25
Peekay Stevens (8)	26
James Jewell (8)	26
Jordan Thomas & Ben Slater (8)	26
Charlotte Williamson (9)	27
Katie Hind (9)	27
Luke Burnhams (8)	27
Euan Cummings (8)	28
Aidan Bappoo (8)	28
Emily Waterfield (9)	28
Alex Ladbrook (8) & Liam Haxton (9)	29
Megan Grover & Carey Faint (8)	29
Katie Riches & Sophie Martin (9)	29
Autumn Dellaway (10)	30
Sam Jones (9)	30
Sarah Millyard (9)	31
Georgia Shearwood (9)	31
Erin Homer (10)	32
Elizabeth Jarvis (10)	32
Beatrice Waters (9)	33
Nathan Hawker (9)	33
Michael Harris (10)	34
Lilah Matthews (9)	35

Mason Lambert (10) 36
Amelia Waters (10) 37
James Mapley (11) 38
Charlotte McCarthy (11) 39
Jeannie Forrester (9) 39
Katie Hurst (11) 40
Kelly Clarke (10) 40
Julia McGee-Russell (9) 41
Jessie Beard (10) 41

Great Ballard School, Eartham
Max Fletcher (9) 42

Harlands CP School, Haywards Heath
Emily Dell (11) 43
Arran Pack (10) 44
Emily Stokes (9) 45
Tasha Jardine (10) 45
Emma Holyer (10) 46
Kate Woodhams (9) 46
Holly Tasker (10) 47
Sarah-Louise Lane (10) 47

Milton Mount Primary School, Crawley
Thomas Owen (9) 48
Shannon Murdoch (8) 48
Greg Morris (9) 49
Noah Twine (8) 49
Hollie Martin (9) 50
Stuart Beed 50
Stewart Feasby (8) 51
Naseem Bouchhar (8) 51
Bethany Gray (8) 52
Billy Towning (8) 52
Theo Ray (8) 53
Jonathan Comber (8) 53
Max Pollock (8) 54
Amy Young (9) 54
Luis Cousillas (9) 55
Kobe Rice (9) 55
Brooke Webb (10) 55

John Ward (10) 56
Antonia Davis (10) 56
Tommy May (9) 56
Alice Lloyd (9) 57
Eva Monoghan Moore (9) 57
Rahel Miah (10) 57
Jack Chappell (9) 58
Ellie Fisher (9) 58
Ella Marsh (9) 58
Joshua Benham (8) 59

Rudgwick Primary School, Horsham
Vicky Ward (9) 60

St Andrew's CE Primary School, Hove
Yakira Traub (11) 61
Elliot Meeten (11) 61
Gabrielle Rickman (11) 62
Tom O'Donnell (10) 62
Holly Phillips (11) 63
Bessie Phiri (11) 63
Eden Townend (10) 64
Josie Kemp (11) 65
Bethany Swindells (11) 66
Tom Fookes (10) 67
Nia Healey Lewis (10) 68
Georgina Cairns (10) 69
Josh Freed (11) 70
Sammy Martin (10) 71
Max Gardiner (10) 72
Declan Brewster (11) 72
Thomas Egeler (10) 73
Oscar Reed (11) 73
Hannah Potterton (11) 74
Florence Norgate (11) 75
Lucy Kirby (11) 76
Alice Grant (11) 77
Clarissa Standen (10) 78
Ellie Homewood (11) 79
Jessie Ward (10) 80
William Walsh (11) 81

Hannah Corcoran (10) 82
Katie Dinnage (10) 83
Martha Borrow (11) 84
Ellie Barnham (11) 85
Amber Van Day (10) 86
Veronica Zambon (11) 87
Louis Alexander (10) 88
Sam French (11) 89
Siobhan Stack-Maddox (11) 90
Rémi Lord (11) 90
Agbude Eseoghene (11) 91
Charlotte Ward (10) 91
Ashleigh Cosham (11) 92

Saltdean CP School, Saltdean
Matthew Clifford (8) 92
Toby Corner (8) 92
Olivia Turner (9) 93
Olivia Bowman (9) 93
Danielle Long (9) 93
Alina Vincent (8) 94
Summer Tyrrell (8) 94
Sophie Walker (9) 94
Alexandra Black (9) 95
Amy Perkins (9) 95
Tegan Jackson (8) 95
Connie Savage (8) 96
Shirley Marchant (8) 96
Dane Lind (8) 96
Jake Lind (8) 97
Oliver Turner (9) 97
Charlotte Cooke (9) 97
Vita Smith (8) 98
Suzannah Gilburt (8) 98
Elizabeth Golding (8) 98
Lucy Rodgers (8) 99
Peter Sowerby (8) 99
Sidney Mohns (9) 100
Mia Ross (8) 100
Connor Lawday (9) 100
Liliana Salih-Miller (8) 101

Thomas Milne (9) 101
Daniel Fernell (8) 101
Evan Ridley (8) 102
Bethany Leak (9) 102
Guy Bolton (9) 102
Ethan Walker (8) 103
Jack Buckingham (9) 103
Oskar Jones (8) 103
Stella O'Neil (8) 104
Lea Donovan (8) 104
Karni Jury (9) 105

West Park CE Middle School, Worthing
Frazer Earl (10) 105
Jessica Battell (9) 106
Sophie Bishop (9) 106
Ryan Sopp & Kristian Binns (9) 107
Abigail Else (9) 107
Joshua Borgars (8) 108
Katherine Germaine & Mia Walton (9) 108
Taylor McGuire (10) 109
Samuel Empson (9) 109
Iyesha Adebisi (8) 110
Elise Price (9) 110
Tabbie Earl (9) 110
Rebecca Hoibak (9) 111
Hannah Boyle (10) 111
Sam Cummings (9) 112
Lewis Amesbury-Fuller (9) 112
Tristan Martin (9) 112
Lauren Bromley (10) 113
Tiffany Watson (9) 113
Kristen Hughes (9) 113
Emily Scott (9) 114
Eleanor Leach (10) 114
Amy Goacher (10) 115
Kate Davies (9) 115
Kathryn Reynolds (9) 116

Freja Coombes (10) 117
Cameron Huggins (10) 117
Jacob Pennels (9) 118
Matthew Lay (10) 119

The Poems

Snow . . .

Amazed that my mum hadn't told me before,

Scraping of cars is the only sound, in this silent world,
No colour in the world except for white,
Outside it's too cold for my fingers to feel,
Winter is here, the first snow in England,
You should see our beech tree covered in snow,

Maybe our school will be closed but no . . .
Out we go to get inspired for a poem,
Rolling the snow to make giant balls,
Now I feel great, playing with my friends,
Inside I feel warm, we make a caterpillar,
Now the balls of snow are heavy, now we are inside,
'Good poem Amelia,' my teacher says.

Amelia Young (10)
Ashurst CE (A) Primary School, Ashurst

Planes

Rushing, shooting through the air,
Pilots concentrating with a stare,
Looking out the cockpit with a glare,
People looking out the window saying, 'Look over there,'
Children squabbling shouting, 'That's not fair.'

Gliding

Slowly gliding through the breeze,
Looking down at all the leaves,
The engine as silent as lots of still trees,
Enjoying the sights of the deep blue seas,
And then the long straight runway the pilot sees.

Sam Wadman (10)
Ashurst CE (A) Primary School, Ashurst

Journey Down The River

Source
A single trickle of water,
Slithers down a lonely rock,
Fresh clean water,
Longing, waiting, wanting to move on,
Suddenly he finds a path,
Running rapidly with a mind of his own,
He crashes down a thunderous waterfall,
Then slushes in a dippy gorge.

Middle
With tranquillity he moves on,
Conquering the land ahead,
Forming a meander,
He finds a shortcut
And leaves an oxbow behind,
He moves through the murky water glistening,
Longing, waiting, wanting to move on.

Mouth
Searching he moves on,
Smelling the salty air he is close,
Silt blossoms in the murky water,
He rampages the banks of the river,
Expanding as he goes,
Searching for the ocean,
He crawls up the sand banks,
Still growing,
Then before his eyes, the vast gigantic mass of sea,
No more longing, waiting, wanting,
He has made it.

Lottie Arnold (10)
Ashurst CE (A) Primary School, Ashurst

A River's Journey

The microscopic trickle of water, starting up the river,
Flows into puddles, then glides slowly on,
Water as clear as glass, thundering current,
Arms flailing, making bubbles,
Waterfalls dropping down,
Racing to reach the family,
Making rocks feel smooth, as it grows ever larger,
Sliding through valleys, getting faster, faster, faster,
Shimmering in the bright yellow sun.

Curving, bending, more meanders,
Picked-up stones are dropped,
Conquering the land ahead,
Picking up friends as it goes along,
Twigs and stones get thrown around corners,
Serenely winding, meandering this way and that,
Escaping branches hailing a lift,
It now takes them on its way,
The river is still glistening in the bright yellow sun.

Wider, wider, on it goes, almost there,
Fresh and saltwater getting mixed,
Creeping silently up what was a small beach,
Rapidly reaching out to win the race,
Seaweed caught at the side,
Yes!
We've made it, we're here,
But still the river is glistening in the bright yellow sun.

Charlotte Bridger (11)
Ashurst CE (A) Primary School, Ashurst

Snow

I wake up on a Wednesday morning,
Feeling very tired,
Might as well lie in, don't feel very inspired!

My mum comes in nagging me,
Trying to get me dressed,
I heard her say something surprising,
Is that really what she said?

It's snowing! It's snowing!
The joy is running through me,
Snow is dripping off the trees,
Dissolving on my tongue.

My feet are really freezing, they're never going to thaw,
I hear Mum calling for breakfast,
But that is such a bore!

I'd rather be . . .
Ducking, sliding through the snow,
Now I know,
I don't want to go to school!

But, out on the school field,
I'm having lots of fun,
The sound of crunching snow,
Echoes in my eardrum!

I wake up the next morning,
Jumping out of bed,
Will the snow still be there?
Happy thoughts come into my head.

Olivia Middleton (10)
Ashurst CE (A) Primary School, Ashurst

Journey Down The River

A pool of water
Stood still in its trap
Suddenly a burst of water
Comes crashing through the rocks
As clear as a crystal
Current getting faster
River meeting its first waterfall
River smoothing the rocks
River getting wider and wider
Cutting through the v-shaped valleys.

Tranquil river meandering
Like a slithering snake
Throwing twigs and stones
From bank to bank
Eating away at the land around it
Conquering the land around it
But the river getting murkier.

River still getting wider
You can smell the sea air
Seaweed flowing in
Freshwater meets saltwater
Tidal water getting sandy
At last the river
Reaches his long lost friend
The river turns to sea.

Harry Fuggles (10)
Ashurst CE (A) Primary School, Ashurst

Puppies Pounce Playfully (Rap)

Little puppies over here,
Lots of puppies everywhere.
Growing big, staying small,
But my pups are the best of all.

Puppies pounce playfully

Bob and Bay in the park,
Scaring children when they bark.
Chewing shoes, ripping hats,
Chasing big hairy cats.

Puppies pounce playfully

Alsatians,
Dalmatians,
Red setter,
Bed wetter
Rat terrier,
All the merrier,
I love them all!

Flori Pearcey (11)
Ashurst CE (A) Primary School, Ashurst

I Am Missing . . .

I am missing,
My caring friends and the fun we had together,
My kind, friendly neighbours,
The brilliant garden, small and unique,
The silent loneliness of winter,
And the bright happiness of birds chirping perkily in the summer,

My bedroom, as cosy as a pair of fluffy slippers,
My warm bed,
My refuge,
The comforting muffled sound of cars going past,

The doggy smell of my conservatory,
The well-loved dog toys, really smelly,
The old worn carpet, as soft as feathers on my feet,

The short walk to the shops,
The kind butcher giving out lollipops,
And I really don't like the thought of someone else
in *my* house!

Rebecca van Pelt (10)
Ashurst CE (A) Primary School, Ashurst

One Snowy Day

I hear my mum call, 'It's snowing, it's snowing!'
One icy Wednesday morning
I jump out of bed
Leap to the window
To find sparkling lumps of snow
That big elephant's my trampoline
That small snowman's my chair
But I cannot recognise
That thing over there.

Crunching of footsteps
Scraping of ice
No chirping of birds
No buzzing of bees
Look out the window
There's snow on the trees.

Starved of sunlight
Through the day
Hands stiff in my gloves
My toes are frozen
Not to mention my feet
The snow's like the blanket which I am under.
Then I fall to sleep while I wonder
Will the snow melt while I'm asleep?

Gabrielle Williams (9)
Ashurst CE (A) Primary School, Ashurst

Rapping Turtles

Turtles swim in the big blue sea,
Bet you don't know where they could be

They swim to the beat
In the big blue sea,
Learning to rap
Very lo-ud-ly

Turtles swim in the big blue sea
Bet you don't know where they could be

I know of a turtle called Turtle 3
Who used to swim in the big blue sea,
Then he saw the rap class on the sea floor
He began to sing rap with his big jaw

When he first began,
This is what he sang,

I'm a rap turtle, turtle rap,
Rapping through the rap, rap, rap,
I roll and rap and rap and roll,
Rapping through the rap, rap, rap.

Joe Homshaw (11)
Ashurst CE (A) Primary School, Ashurst

Rain Storm

The light pattering of rain splashing on the
hard crusty ground.
The crystal clear water slowly falling from the sky,
gracefully gliding down like a bird.

The rain slowly getting stronger as it
shoots out of the clouds.
The small puddles growing bigger and bigger,
more and more ripples appear.

The rain starts to get lighter and the mist is starting to clear
and a big colourful rainbow emerges from the skies above,
the clouds fade away.
Beams of light come down to dry up the earth.

Charlie Nunn (10)
Ashurst CE (A) Primary School, Ashurst

Babyhood is . . .

A new leaf unfolding slowly and gently
From a tiny bud
In the bright days of spring

Childhood is . . .
A dazzling sunny summer day
With bees buzzing and a fresh cool breeze
Flowing over a field

Adulthood is . . .
A flock of busy birds
Awkwardly flying over
Green grassy hills

Old age is . . .
A gloomy autumn evening
With leaves falling from trees
And colourful plants dying.

Douglas Ford (11)
Ashurst CE (A) Primary School, Ashurst

The Cricketer's Rap

There was a cricket player in a cricket match,
and when the batsman hit the ball he made his catch.
When they saw he caught the ball the crowd went clap,
and when they did he took off his
cricket cap.

Cricket player,
cricket player in a match,
cricket player,
cricket player makes his catch.

Cricket player name Steve Gatting,
cricket player next in batting,
when it is his turn to bat,
he gives the ball a mighty smack.
When they see him
smack the ball,
they then shout out,
'You're so cool.'

Cricket player,
cricket player goes to bat,
cricket player,
cricket player,
Howzat!

Robert Loveless (9)
Ashurst CE (A) Primary School, Ashurst

Excited

Excited is like you have butterflies in your tummy.
Excited feels like happy times.
Excited tastes like chocolate cake.
Excited reminds you of your birthday.
Excited sounds like screaming
Excited is the colour red.

Danielle Golding (8)
Bishop Tufnell Junior School, Bognor Regis

Lonely

Lonely is like . . . you are on your own.
What colour is it?
White
Lonely smells like . . . smoky air
What does it sound like?
A twister spinning.
Lonely feels like . . . your heart is broken.

Sophie Turner (9)
Bishop Tufnell Junior School, Bognor Regis

Sadness

Sadness feels like you have been killed
Sadness is smelly like sick
Sadness reminds me of nightmares
Sadness sounds like babies crying
Sadness looks like a person dying
Sadness tastes like salty water
Sadness is blue like a raging river.

Danny Cooper (8)
Bishop Tufnell Junior School, Bognor Regis

Anger

Anger reminds me of getting cross.
Anger is the colour red.
Anger sounds like a gunshot fired.
Anger smells like a pile of mushy blood.
Anger looks like a robber stealing money.
Anger tastes like pure evil.
Anger feels like being thrown in the sea.

Joshua Leslie (8)
Bishop Tufnell Junior School, Bognor Regis

Love

Love is the colour of pink.
Love reminds me of a baby as sweet as honey.
Love sounds like children laughing.
Love smells like fresh strawberries.
Love looks like a flower bed.
Love tastes like a sugar lump.
Love feels like hair that has just been washed.

Jessica Dawling (8)
Bishop Tufnell Junior School, Bognor Regis

Laughter

Laughter feels lively.
Laughter smells like sweets.
Laughter reminds me of good times.
Laughter sounds like a sweet boy singing.
Laughter looks like a beautiful red flower.
Laughter is the colour yellow.

Zak Boniface (9)
Bishop Tufnell Junior School, Bognor Regis

Anger

Anger is red like hot steel.
Anger reminds me of the sun burning red-hot.
Anger sounds like roaring wind.
Anger smells like hot red smoke.
Anger looks like a burning forest.
Anger tastes like red blood.

Ceara Rumsey (8)
Bishop Tufnell Junior School, Bognor Regis

Love

Love tastes like a box full of chocolates.
Love feels like someone's given you a big hug.
Love smells like a bed of freshly cut roses.
Love reminds me of my first Valentine's Day.
Love sounds like music playing.
Love looks like two doves flying in a sunlit sky.
Love is red like a beating heart.

Georgia Stevens (8)
Bishop Tufnell Junior School, Bognor Regis

Love

Love is red like a heart-shaped pillow.
Love tastes like a glass of red wine.
Love feels like your first wedding.
Love smells like chocolate floating in the air.
Love reminds me of a boyfriend.
Love sounds like loads of bells ringing.
Love looks like two people kissing.

Emma Last (8)
Bishop Tufnell Junior School, Bognor Regis

Laughter

Laughter sounds like the tinkling of bells.
Laughter smells like green meadows and mint.
Laughter looks like a golden angel.
Laughter tastes like sweet sugar.
Laughter reminds me of rays of sunlight.
Laughter feels like the smoothest silk.
Laughter is golden, as bright as the sun.

Julia McGee-Russell (9)
Bishop Tufnell Junior School, Bognor Regis

Frightened

Frightened is white.
Frightened is like you are lost.
Frightened looks like tears running down your cheek.
Frightened is like your heart is being ripped out.
Frightened sounds like tyres screeching.

Elliot Playle-Howard (9)
Bishop Tufnell Junior School, Bognor Regis

Calm

Calm is as blue as a river.
Calm tastes like a lollipop.
Calm smells like perfume.
Calm feels like Hariboes.
Calm reminds me of a flat sea.

Cameron Cousens (9)
Bishop Tufnell Junior School, Bognor Regis

Hate

Hate is dark like a cloud.
Hate reminds me of sadness.
Hate tastes like lava running down my neck.
Hate looks like a cold hard demon.

Bradley Dodman (8)
Bishop Tufnell Junior School, Bognor Regis

Fun

Fun is the colour of blue.
Fun reminds me of the beach.
Fun sounds like people laughing.
Fun smells like perfume.
Fun looks like giggling children.
Fun tastes like candy.
Fun feels like you're being tickled.

Alana Kirkpatrick (8)
Bishop Tufnell Junior School, Bognor Regis

Laughter

Laughter is the colour blue.
Laughter is sweet.
Laughter tastes like fresh water.
Laughter reminds me of a roller coaster.
Laughter looks like sweets.
Laughter feels like the sky.

Jacob Lowery (8)
Bishop Tufnell Junior School, Bognor Regis

Happy

Happy tastes like Hariboes.
Happy feels like you're buying seven pets.
Happy reminds me of my very own pet.
Happy smells like a birthday cake.

Bradley Atkins (8)
Bishop Tufnell Junior School, Bognor Regis

Frightened

Frightened is black like coal.
Frightened sounds like screaming.
Frightened smells like spicy pepper.
Frightened feels like being sick.
Frightened reminds me of my sad days.

Daniel Cox (8)
Bishop Tufnell Junior School, Bognor Regis

Fun

Fun is orange
Fun is like a singing bird
Fun smells like a sugar sweet
Fun tastes like popping bubblegum
Fun sounds like people laughing
Fun feels like a sun shining bright
Fun reminds me of my mum's perfume.

Jade Longworth (8)
Bishop Tufnell Junior School, Bognor Regis

Fun

Fun is yellow like the sunshine,
Fun smells like candles all lit up,
Fun tastes like fresh apples,
Fun sounds like bells ringing,
Fun feels like silk,
Fun reminds me of playing with my friends.

Demi Rishman (9)
Bishop Tufnell Junior School, Bognor Regis

Calm

Calm is yellow like sand
Calm tastes like chips
Calm looks like the beach
Calm smells like chilli
Calm sounds like calm waves
Calm feels like a bed
Calm reminds me of happiness.

Ashley Walpole (8)
Bishop Tufnell Junior School, Bognor Regis

Sadness

Sadness is black like ashes,
Sadness smells like rotting apples,
Sadness looks like a lava stream,
Sadness tastes like coal,
Sadness sounds like thunder,
Sadness feels like rain,
Sadness reminds me of torture.

Dean Edwards (9)
Bishop Tufnell Junior School, Bognor Regis

Love

Love is pink like hearts,
Love looks like love hearts,
Love is the smell of fish and chips,
Love tastes like a BBQ,
Love sounds like birds singing,
Love feels like a new beginning,
Love reminds me of perfume.

Samuel Baker (9)
Bishop Tufnell Junior School, Bognor Regis

Happiness

Happiness is yellow like fun.
Happiness sounds like a football going into the net.
Happiness looks like someone cheering.
Happiness reminds me of jumping.
Happiness feels like a comfy chair.
Happiness tastes like chips.
Happiness smells like leather seats in a convertible.

Ross Edwards (8)
Bishop Tufnell Junior School, Bognor Regis

Excited

Excited is golden like a Christmas decoration.
Excited smells like chips cooking.
Excited looks like a pile of birthday presents for me.
Excited tastes like a bar of creamy chocolate.
Excited sounds like happy children playing.
Excited feels like going to Disneyland.
Excited reminds me of my family and my friends.

Beatrice Waters (9)
Bishop Tufnell Junior School, Bognor Regis

Anger

Anger is red like lava
Anger smells of egg
Anger looks like red poo
Anger tastes like blood
Anger sounds like thunder
Anger feels like mud
Anger reminds me of the bad times I've had.

Kyra Beaven (8)
Bishop Tufnell Junior School, Bognor Regis

Lonely

Lonely is yellow like ducks,
Lonely smells like bananas,
Lonely looks like the world,
Lonely tastes like salt,
Lonely sounds like crying,
Lonely feels like sand,
Lonely reminds me of having no friends.

Eloise Kenchington (8)
Bishop Tufnell Junior School, Bognor Regis

Silence

Silence is white like paper.
Silence feels like air.
Silence tastes like hot chocolate.
Silence looks like a clean ocean.
Silence reminds me of losing my rabbit.
Silence sounds like a clear sky.

Jack Hawkins (8)
Bishop Tufnell Junior School, Bognor Regis

Excited

Excited is lilac like a butterfly flapping,
Excited smells like fish and chips,
Excited looks like someone jumping up and down,
Excited tastes like party food,
Excited sounds like someone screaming,
Excited feels like fun,
Excited reminds me of joy.

Maisie Fleming (8)
Bishop Tufnell Junior School, Bognor Regis

Peacefulness

Peacefulness is yellow,
Peacefulness smells like a world of flowers,
Peacefulness looks like rabbits eating grass in a meadow,
Peacefulness tastes like fruit lollipops,
Peacefulness sounds like birds tweeting,
Peacefulness feels like God touching you,
Peacefulness reminds me of rainbows over the sea.

Ezra Whitlock (8)
Bishop Tufnell Junior School, Bognor Regis

Worried

Worried is white.
Worried smells like saltwater.
Worried tastes like onions.
Worried sounds like a lion.
Worried feels like an egg.
Worried reminds me of being seasick.

Paige Whiting (9)
Bishop Tufnell Junior School, Bognor Regis

Calm

Calmness is like the clouds.
Calmness smells like cheese on toast,
Calmness looks like my Game Boy,
Calmness tastes like a hamburger,
Calmness sounds like Sam S,
Calmness feels like my Game Boy,
Calmness reminds me of the beach.

Jacob White (9)
Bishop Tufnell Junior School, Bognor Regis

Sadness

Sadness is black like death
Sadness reminds me of bullying
Sadness tastes like chillies
Sadness looks like blood
Sadness feels like being stabbed
Sadness sounds like crying
Sadness smells like old perfume.

David Harris (8)
Bishop Tufnell Junior School, Bognor Regis

A Poem About Love

Love is red like a sunset.
Love is happy like sweet dreams.
Love is as sweet as candy.
Love reminds me of puppy-dogs.
Love feels like a big hug.
Love smells like candyfloss.
Love looks like fluffy white clouds in the sky.

Kelsey Brooke (8)
Bishop Tufnell Junior School, Bognor Regis

Worried

Worried is pale blue like a lonely wave,
Worried smells like seaweed,
Worried looks like a crying child,
Worried tastes like a bitter lemon,
Worried sounds like cawing seagulls,
Worried feels like squelching mud,
Worried reminds me of handing my homework in late.

Lilah Matthews (9)
Bishop Tufnell Junior School, Bognor Regis

Happiness

Happiness looks like a dancing teddy bear
Multicoloured is the colour of the rainbow
That is ginormous as can be
Happiness reminds me of my holidays.
Happiness is like a smooth, gentle car driving across.
Happiness smells like my favourite dinner.

Jade Fox (9)
Bishop Tufnell Junior School, Bognor Regis

A Poem About Sadness

Sadness is pink like a pig's ear.
Sadness looks like a bare tree swaying in the breeze.
Sadness looks like salty tears.
Sadness feels like a dead river.
Sadness reminds me of my great granny.

Beth Clarke (9)
Bishop Tufnell Junior School, Bognor Regis

Love

Love feels like a fluffy cloud above singing birds.
Love is as pink as a pig.
Love reminds me of butterflies flying high.
Love looks like crystal diamonds in the crystal clear sea.
Love smells like candyfloss from a funfair.

Dina Betsworth (8)
Bishop Tufnell Junior School, Bognor Regis

Sadness

Sadness is like crystal-blue tears.
Sadness looks like a bare tree.
Sadness reminds me of a sinking boat with a million lives on board.
Sadness feels like bolts going down my back.
Sadness smells like salty tears and vinegar.

Giorgia Cappella (9)
Bishop Tufnell Junior School, Bognor Regis

A Poem About Sadness

Sadness is the colour blue like a thunderous storm.
Sadness looks like a plain, brown, bare tree.
Sadness reminds me of being bullied.
Sadness feels like ice-cold rain.
Sadness smells like strong, salty vinegar.

Megan Lewis (8)
Bishop Tufnell Junior School, Bognor Regis

Love Poem

Love is like red roses among frosty morning dew.
Love is like a dazzling crystal shimmering in the sun.
Love feels like sitting on pure white fluffy clouds.
Love smells like rich perfume in the mild morning springs.
Love reminds me of the calm fresh ocean.

Ella Frye (8)
Bishop Tufnell Junior School, Bognor Regis

Fear - Haikus

Fear is dull dark black
Like a dark stormy landscape
Shadows surround me.

Fear feels like blazing
Hot lava down your T-shirt
Lava frightens me.

Fear smells like red-hot
Chilli peppers on my plate
They smell disgusting.

Joe Benjamin & Josh Clark (9)
Bishop Tufnell Junior School, Bognor Regis

Love

Love is like church bells ringing.
Love is like the birds that are singing.
Love is like the morning sun.
Love is proud like a fluffy cloud.
Love is like a cheering crowd.
Love reminds me of a loud sound.
Love smells like a baker's bun.

Josh Markey (9) & Ross Stephenson-Gill (8)
Bishop Tufnell Junior School, Bognor Regis

Sadness

Sadness is like blue volcano tears bursting out.
Sadness looks like people in a war.
Sadness reminds me of my grandad dying of old age.
Sadness smells like onions that make you cry.

Paige Knight (8)
Bishop Tufnell Junior School, Bognor Regis

Anger

Anger reminds me of snapping crocodiles in Africa.
Anger reminds me of rampaging elephants in the Masai Mara
Anger looks like a gyle goblin with an ugly body.
Anger is red like running molten lava
Dribbling out of the mouth of the volcano.
Anger smells like a stink bomb going off down the hallway.
Anger feels like poison ivy all over your body.

Peekay Stevens (8)
Bishop Tufnell Junior School, Bognor Regis

Anger

Anger smells like socks found under the bed.
Anger is red like a burning fire.
Anger reminds me of the sorrow of a loved one.
Anger looks like Hell.
Anger feels like people crying.

James Jewell (8)
Bishop Tufnell Junior School, Bognor Regis

Sadness

Sadness is as blue as a rough sea.
Sadness looks like a scream.
Sadness feels prickly like a porcupine.
Sadness smells like pouring rain.
Sadness reminds me of ice melting.

Jordan Thomas & Ben Slater (8)
Bishop Tufnell Junior School, Bognor Regis

Anger

Anger tastes like hot chillies melting in your mouth
Anger feels like a volcano erupting in my hands
Anger smells like a house on fire burning into ashes
Anger reminds me of the sun's hot rays
Anger sounds like crackling fireworks demolishing in the sky
Anger looks like a lion pouncing on me
Anger is the colour of burning-hot fiery red.

Charlotte Williamson (9)
Bishop Tufnell Junior School, Bognor Regis

Love

Love is as red as a rose.
Love reminds me of happiness.
Love sounds like a song from the sweetest songbird.
Love smells like the tallest sunflower that grows.
Love looks like the garden covered in snow.
Love tastes like honey in a pot.
Love feels like the fluffiest cat you ever did see.

Katie Hind (9)
Bishop Tufnell Junior School, Bognor Regis

Scared

Scared is red like a lion.
Scared feels like my heart is beating.
Scared smells like someone just went to the toilet.

Luke Burnhams (8)
Bishop Tufnell Junior School, Bognor Regis

Anger

Anger reminds me of my brother snatching the controller off me.
Anger sounds like the sea crashing into the coast.
Anger smells like burning food.
Anger looks like bubbling hot fire and lava.
Anger tastes like phlegm.
Anger feels like a grip on your neck.
Anger is the colour red.

Euan Cummings (8)
Bishop Tufnell Junior School, Bognor Regis

Anger

Anger is horrible.
Anger is cursed, it is like the Devil has got you in his hands.
Anger is like a grip on a gun.
Anger looks like burning fire.
Anger tastes like sick.
Anger smells like rotting flesh.
Anger reminds me of when my dad got paralysed.
Anger is bright crimson but stay away from it because it is nasty.

Aidan Bappoo (8)
Bishop Tufnell Junior School, Bognor Regis

Anger

Anger reminds me of a house on fire.
Anger sounds like a cat's claws scraping on a blackboard.
Anger smells like burning plastic.
Anger looks like a volcano erupting.
Anger tastes like a sour plum.
Anger feels like a sharp rock.
Anger is the colour of burning-hot chilli-red.

Emily Waterfield (9)
Bishop Tufnell Junior School, Bognor Regis

Happiness

Happiness looks like colourful butterflies flying in the open
Happiness feels like a rose-red ladybird
Happiness smells like lavender
Happiness looks like people laughing and having fun.

Alex Ladbrook (8) & Liam Haxton (9)
Bishop Tufnell Junior School, Bognor Regis

Fear - Haikus

Fear reminds me of,
A violent crashing sea,
Which blows me away.

Fear is pollution
Smelling like oil and petrol,
I want to escape.

Fear is navy blue,
Like a dark, stormy seascape,
Crashing against rocks.

Fear looks icy cold,
Like a misty blue morning
Chilling my old bones.

Megan Grover & Carey Faint (8)
Bishop Tufnell Junior School, Bognor Regis

Fear - Haiku

Fear is misty grey
Like a crashing rough sea that,
Could blow you away.

Katie Riches & Sophie Martin (9)
Bishop Tufnell Junior School, Bognor Regis

Scared And Alone

She was in the woods,
Scared and alone.
The moon so bright in the starlit sky,
Badgers playing mischievously by the old decaying trees.
Frosted ivy creeping, suffocating long delicate branches.
Green fungi growing, eating soft firm bark,
No sound of the friendly owl,
Only the harsh whispering wind.
She was in the woods,
Scared and alone.

Autumn Dellaway (10)
Bishop Tufnell Junior School, Bognor Regis

A Fox At Rest

I climbed slowly out of my burrow
The smell of open air hit my nostrils.
I moved right out of my hole
Leaves under my feet crunched,
Fungi stood firm in the ground
I was in the frightening woods
The scent of rotted trees hung around me
I was cold;
I was scared . . .
Haunted twisted trees everywhere
The owl hooted;
The wolf howled;
A twig snapped;
I turned around
There was my home
I scurried inside
And I was safe at last.
A fox at rest.

Sam Jones (9)
Bishop Tufnell Junior School, Bognor Regis

The Woods In The Deep

Down in the woods, the muddiest woods,
The birds sing in the trees.
I can feel the damp, damp bark
Crunch beneath my feet.
Down in the woods, the murkiest woods,
I can feel the mist surround me.

My boots sink deep
As I squelch through the mud.
Down in the woods, the deepest woods.
Dark, deep trees surround me.
As I look up in the clearing
I find daylight and I know I have been dreaming.

Sarah Millyard (9)
Bishop Tufnell Junior School, Bognor Regis

The Deep, Dark Woods

I love winter.
It's peaceful and calm
I'm in the woods,
The deep, dark woods
And tall trees
That surround me.
I'm relaxed in the woods,
The deep, dark woods
Because nature is around me.

I hear bark snapping while I walk
Squelch, squelch
Through the muddiest swamp.
I'm lonely in the woods,
The deep, dark woods,
Because nature is sleeping.

Georgia Shearwood (9)
Bishop Tufnell Junior School, Bognor Regis

Deep In The Woods

Deep in the woods,
Where the oak trees stand,
I see some huntsmen on the farmer's land,
I watch them from a distance as they all seem to flock,
I look away in horror and it fills me with shock.

A loud yelp in the distance as the vixen draws near,
I was soon to realise that her baby had died
And she was shedding a tear.

All the creatures around me hurrying by,
The fear in their faces nearly made me cry.
The silence was instant with no creatures around,
Just me on my own deep in the woods where the oak trees stand.

Erin Homer (10)
Bishop Tufnell Junior School, Bognor Regis

The Bluebell Woods

Bluebell Woods,
Winter is ending,
What were dark silhouettes of the bare trees,
Are now vibrant green towers of life,
Which reach up to the golden sun shining over the woods,
At their feet lies a sweet-smelling carpet of purple bluebells,
All you can hear is the spring breeze rustling the leaves,
The birds singing and the insects humming,
Whilst the sunbeams dance across the breathtaking flowers,
It is such a magical feeling,
So enchanting that many a person would come to visit,
The Bluebell Woods.

Elizabeth Jarvis (10)
Bishop Tufnell Junior School, Bognor Regis

The Woods

I crept through the dark, damp, gloomy woods,
My paws pattering on the wet soil,
The trees were towering above me like giants.

Then, the distant rumble of voices coming closer and closer,
The loud thud of heavy boots. Humans.
As fast as lightning I hid behind a tree,
The noises got louder and louder . . .

Suddenly there they were; lots of them,
Huge figures blocking out the sunlight,
My heart felt like a drum banging in my chest.

I almost flew back to my lair,
The next time I ventured out everything had changed;
The trees no longer towered above me.

In my favourite clearing there were benches to sit on,
There were no wild paths, only one,
The others were cut off by thick tree trunks lying down,
It wasn't my home anymore . . .

Beatrice Waters (9)
Bishop Tufnell Junior School, Bognor Regis

That Night

I heard it that night!
Leaves rustling . . .
I saw it that night!
Fox catching . . .
I felt it that night!
Mist creeping . . .
I sensed it that night!
Danger approaching . . .

Nathan Hawker (9)
Bishop Tufnell Junior School, Bognor Regis

The Woods

The ivy crawled up the towering trees,
While the branches twisted and gnarled.
The dark, leafy canopy covered the light,
And the tree trunks creaked and curled.

The stars glistened in the pitch-black sky,
The moon was a silver balloon.
There wasn't a cloud in the dark velvet night,
No hole in the murky gloom.

Twittering insects hidden in the trees,
Squeaking and scurrying around.
Moss stuck to the rotting boughs,
Bark lay on the ground.

The winding path twisted and turned,
Into the starlit night.
The moon glowed bright high up in the sky,
Giving off a thin sliver of light.

The ivy crawled up the towering trees,
While the branches twisted and gnarled.
The dark, leafy canopy covered the light,
And the tree trunks creaked and curled.

Michael Harris (10)
Bishop Tufnell Junior School, Bognor Regis

Did They See Me?

Did they see me?
I crept through the woods,
My heart was beating like a drum,
I saw them wandering in my woods near my den,
They carried their axes over their shoulders,
Their axes glinted like a new key.

Did they see me?
I let out a startled cry,
I turned and scampered behind some trees.
The woods suddenly seemed spookier than before . . .
I hid behind a tree and they walked past,
Their axes held high.

Did they see me?
I looked all round, I couldn't see anything except the people,
They were cutting down trees,
They were destroying my world,
Getting nearer and nearer to my home.
Panic filled my body like water in a jug,
I had to warn my family. I darted across the path
In front of the men

Did they see me; did they care!

Lilah Matthews (9)
Bishop Tufnell Junior School, Bognor Regis

Something About The Woods

There's something about the woods.
All alone surrounded by God's magic.
Peace and quiet in my solitaire moods.
No worries, people or events so tragic.

Crisp, cool air in my lungs.
The whisper of forest breeze.
A break from climbing life's rungs.
A special time on my memory to freeze.

A paradise of contentment,
To restore my soul's energy.
No worry about advancement.
Basking in nature's sweet synergy.

No more of life's fast frame.
Back in control of my time.
Each day not more of the same.
Money no issue. I don't need a dime.

There's something about the woods.
Only here can real peace be found.
Not a crowded neighbourhood,
Where all is one busy, loud sound.

Nothing can compare to starlit canopy.
A hot steaming cup of camper's tea.
The preservation of my sanity.
I escape from life's endless sea . . .

Mason Lambert (10)
Bishop Tufnell Junior School, Bognor Regis

The Woods

Golden-brown leaves are a clump of small bees,
Swarming the wizened trees.
Twisted, gnarled and knotted,
Forever climbing upwards.

Cool shady patches, the rustling leaves block the sunbeams
Filtering down on a cushy carpet of leaves.
A ripple across the shimmering, sparkling lake.
The woods teem with wildlife.

In summer there is a radiant blue sky
And fluffy candyfloss clouds.
A young blackbird soars in the sunlight,
Singing as it flies, happy and carefree.

And then the moon glows luminous
In the dark velvety sky,
A warm breeze still blows,
The twinkling stars shine like jewels.

In colder months, glittering icicles
Crowd the bare trees, sharp yet pretty.
A soft white blanket covers the ground
And crunches of feet have dissolved into silence.

Sometimes colourful flowers bloom and baby lambs leap up
Animals appear, a warm shower
Of glistening raindrops fall
But even in the different months . . .
The wood will always be beautiful.

Amelia Waters (10)
Bishop Tufnell Junior School, Bognor Regis

What Happened To The Boy?

It was a dark and murky night,
The boy was walking through the woods,
As he was walking he saw fungus growing off the decaying and rotting tree.

As he walked further and further into the woods he saw microscopic icicles hanging off the delicate leaves,
The ground was covered in a thick layer of mud that was moist and had frozen in the early hours of the night.

He walked and walked until he could go no further,
Through the mountains of layers of branches and leaves he could see the bright stars that filled the sky,
It looked like someone had spent hours painting them,
They were all so precise and the moon beamed down on him and glistened like a jeweller's shop window filled with perfect diamonds.

It was getting darker and darker as he went deeper and deeper into the eerie woods,
He suddenly heard a terrifying howl,
He looked round and round but he could see nothing but blackness.

He started to run faster and faster,
He could hear footsteps getting closer and closer,
All of a sudden he tripped over a log that had been cut down,
He was face to face with his worst nightmare!

In the depths of the woods one could hear,
A loud scream, then complete silence.

James Mapley (11)
Bishop Tufnell Junior School, Bognor Regis

The Watchers Of The Wood

The men came riding, riding,
On a chilly winter night.
The moon was a torch in the sky,
That lit up the forest floor.

The men came riding, riding,
On up to the leafy edge;
Where the eyes had a longing stare.

The wind had a howling howl,
When the men came riding, riding,
The animals to scare.

The birds gave a laugh of fear,
The foxes shrunk away,
For it was dark that night,
When the men came riding, riding,
From far, far away . . .

Charlotte McCarthy (11)
Bishop Tufnell Junior School, Bognor Regis

Sadness

Sadness is black like night.
Sadness is like being away from home for a year.
Sadness sounds like a bird screeching.
Sadness smells like a river in a dark forest.
Sadness looks like a blank screen.
Sadness tastes like a stone in the back of your throat.
Sadness feels like someone in your family has died.

Jeannie Forrester (9)
Bishop Tufnell Junior School, Bognor Regis

Emerald Forest

The emerald forest shimmered in the moonlight
As the great oak towered over me
Its cold dead moss sat on the tree
As the sun came out all was bright

The long arm of a tree
Looked like creepy wood decaying in the night
The wind gusted around my feet
And gave me a terrible fright

As I looked all around
I noticed that all the trees had gone
Apart from one
The great oak tree still stands
The emerald forest shimmered in the moonlight.

Katie Hurst (11)
Bishop Tufnell Junior School, Bognor Regis

I Am Here

I am here in the woods,
But I know you can't see me.
I see tall trees towering above me,
And the massive world all around.
When people walk they make
A loud crunch in the bark.
Sometimes the birds sing me
Into a light sleep.
Then more people come
And wake me with their wellies,
Careful! They may stand on me.
I am here in the woods
But no. You can't see me.
Don't worry.
I am just an ant.

Kelly Clarke (10)
Bishop Tufnell Junior School, Bognor Regis

I Am A Robin

I am a little robin and as I build my nest
Snowflakes fall around me, even on my breast.
Ivy climbs above me, making a great wreath,
The grass below is frosty; a fox runs underneath.

The moon shines above me, a huge, great eye.
An owl turns his head around, the wind flies by.
A mouse lifts his head to me; squeaks a loud, 'Hello!'
I warn him of the owl above and the fox below.

With a little, 'Thanks!' he quickly runs away.
He is a little friend of mine, in spring I hope we'll play.
The fox passes by again and says, 'I must implore!'
'I am a vegetarian, I wouldn't harm his paw!'

'Everyone thinks I'm mean and that I'll bite.
But I'm cold and shivering, in this deep, dark night.'
He looks so cold and frightened I welcome him inside
Gratefully he says, 'As you are so kind, I really must abide.'

So that is what has happened in this deep, dark night
I am not so lonely now; I don't have to have a fright!

Julia McGee-Russell (9)
Bishop Tufnell Junior School, Bognor Regis

Poor, Poor Me

Poor, poor me, they don't care,
What I look like, what I wear.
I don't wear many bright colours,
Browns, whites, blacks and some others.
The rustling leaves that surround me,
Show off their looks upon a tree.
But no; I sit all by myself,
They don't even care about my health.
I want to be like most of the others,
I don't even get company from my sisters or brothers.
I sit alone like any other fungus I know,
Wait until I'm stepped upon then I have to go!

Jessie Beard (10)
Bishop Tufnell Junior School, Bognor Regis

Dogs

Big dogs,
Little dogs,
Eenie, weenie, teeny dogs.

Dogs with four legs.

Curly dogs,
Shaggy dogs,
Fluffy pink poodle dogs.

Dogs with wagging tails.

Yappy dogs,
Snappy dogs,
Love you when they're happy dogs.

Dogs with innocent barks.

Talented dogs,
Silly dogs,
Clever dogs that eat your lunch.

Dogs with curious eyes.

Brown dogs,
White dogs,

Dogs with shiny wet noses.

Lap dogs,
Working dogs,
Loud bouncy hunting dogs,
I love dogs.

Max Fletcher (9)
Great Ballard School, Eartham

The River Ride

Crisp and clear
No sound I can hear
On my own
All alone
Just me and the silver ice
Freezing cold, not that nice
Coming to the doors and the land ahead
Time to move to the river bed.

Streaming, whooshing, falling down
Heading towards the city, town
Twirling, whirling, swirling on
See me then, now I'm gone
Speeding, gliding, rushing through
The green valley where the apples grew
Riding past the city now
Towards the countryside and the huge black and white cow,.

Passing farms with woolly sheep
See a horse ready to leap
Flowing forwards down the hill
Passing the big baker's mill
Continuing my journey to reach the sea
Watching it now, yippee, yippee
Spotting the bright, big, blue waves
Hang on a minute, I'm in a daze
Yes, that's it, there it is
Streaming towards it, in a whiz
Farewell, goodbye
Time to lead up to the sky!

Emily Dell (11)
Harlands CP School, Haywards Heath

What Really Happened That Day (On The Boat To Rome)

Some say we fled to another country
Some say we fell overboard
Some say a giant sea monster overturned us
But that's not the story.

Whilst we were sailing a cliff gave way?
No that's not the story
Other crazy things we thought
But it's time the real story was taught.

On the never-ending blue . . .
'Twas time to arrive
But instead of seaside
It was a ghostly silence.

Gliding alongside what we hoped to be seaside
That belonged to home, that home was Rome.
Once we were aware that we knew, not where
We glanced round in despair, this place was so bare.

Idle we were in courage for Mars, God of War
Had sent down here a curse, we could only stare in awe.
But as we looked closer, something glinted in the sand
One of us bravely picked it up, it was a jewel and engraved on it said:
'I've travelled here, it is so bare, brave are thee, to come wandering.'

We had no idea what this message meant
But one thing we knew, whoever had been here had a warning
to be said.
Quickly we got our boat ready, we would have fled
If something else we saw hadn't made us stop.

We saw something else engraved on the back of the jewel:
'Tell others about this island. AM.'
When we found our way home, when our boat had come to port,
Immediately to Caesar we reported.

'We sailed off course to an island so bare.'
Caesar laughed and said, 'Impossible, all islands have been found.'
So we named the place America and hoped too
Like A.M. again, it would be found.

Arran Pack (10)
Harlands CP School, Haywards Heath

Training Barracks

Here I am in a whole new world
Thinking, *where am I, what shall I do?*
Feeling homesick, speechless and all jumpy
It is rather homely but very cold.

I'm in the training barracks
It's so big with 100 rooms
But the snoring in the night, wow
It's creepy, frightening and weird here but it's okay.

Some rooms are hot, some rooms are cold
Noisy and quiet, big and scary
Told off for yawning, it's the other soldier's fault
Quite scared of the chief centurion
I'll get used to it though.

Emily Stokes (9)
Harlands CP School, Haywards Heath

Tiger, Tiger

(Inspired by 'The Tiger' by William Blake)

Tiger, tiger, you are so big and fast
Tiger, tiger, you never ever come last
Tiger, tiger, you have so many stripes
Tiger, tiger, why are you black and white?

Tasha Jardine (10)
Harlands CP School, Haywards Heath

Rough Sea

The waves were clashing, the sea was roaring
There was no going back now
The sea was tumbling over and over us
There was no going back now!

The sky was gloomy, the sea glum
There was no going back now
We sailed on over the waves
As they pounded into us
There was no going back now!

Coming near to land the wave came to a halt
Only no going back now
The sea changed from dim grey to metallic blue and green
No going back now!

Emma Holyer (10)
Harlands CP School, Haywards Heath

Tiger, Tiger

(Inspired by 'The Tiger' by William Blake)

Tiger, tiger, burning bright
Proudly prowling through the night
Prancing up with glaring eyes
Slinking under starlit skies.

I saw him creeping round a bush
Slowly, slowly, step by step
Clenching his teeth, ready to pounce
On a little innocent mouse.

Kate Woodhams (9)
Harlands CP School, Haywards Heath

Burning Orange

(Inspired by 'The Tiger' by William Blake)

Tiger, tiger, shining so bright
With all your fire possessed within
May the flame be immortal
And all the orange, gold and black
Silently lighting the way forth
To be with I so proudly
The breaking of fiery morns
Alight with your precious gold coat
To a sound of ferocious roars
Be eternal in thy flowing sleep
And awake with mournful eyes
Arts of your coat burn in thy mind
Tiger, tiger, could flicker out.

Holly Tasker (10)
Harlands CP School, Haywards Heath

Tiger, Tiger

(Inspired by 'The Tiger' by William Blake)

Tiger, tiger, your teeth so bare,
Your baring fangs so sharp
Tiger, tiger, your slinky steady
Step after step
Tiger, tiger, bare your teeth
Dripping, dropping, plop
Tiger, tiger, your glaring eyes
Staring into your prey.

Sarah-Louise Lane (10)
Harlands CP School, Haywards Heath

On The Ship

On the ship I saw
Colossal waves coming towards us
On the ship I heard
The raging seas forcefully crashing against the sides of the hull
On the ship I smelt
The mouldy stench of the rank pirates
On the ship I felt
The soggy ropes as I climbed the rigging
On the ship I tasted
The excitement as land draws closer
On the ship I cowered in fear
As the ship was whipped by the wind and rain.

Thomas Owen (9)
Milton Mount Primary School, Crawley

On Board A Ship

I taste the salt of the sea on my dainty lips
I can taste the salty tang of the air
I can touch the rigging when I climb it
I can touch the treasure in my hands
I can feel the fright of losing
I can feel the glory of winning
I can hear the clanking of the captain's peg leg
I can hear the howling of the pirates on deck
I can see spilt blood of a pirate
I can see the sails beautifully flowing on a sunny day.

Shannon Murdoch (8)
Milton Mount Primary School, Crawley

Henry Munday, The Child Criminal

I am winter when it is cold and foggy
I am painful boils which everyone wants to get rid of
I am a dirty shirt which is ripped and tattered
I am a decaying fish bone that has been abandoned in the gutter
I am a soulless demolished building that has no life
I am four days hard labour and whipped
I am Henry Munday.

Greg Morris (9)
Milton Mount Primary School, Crawley

My Life On A Pirate Ship

As I stood on a pirate ship's deck
I saw the captain wrenching a rope round a pirate's neck
I saw pirates singing sea shanties
And eating biscuits, wow, they're manky.

As I looked over the side
I heard pirate ships far and wide
I heard roaring waves in the sea
And a clitter-clatter of a pirate's key.

As I slept on the pirate's floor
I smelled old cut wood from a cabin door
I smelled the old stench of creepy weevils
When I smell that smell it gives me evils.

As I stood near the pirate ship's side
I touched the blood, someone must have died
I touched the wooden planks on the floor
They looked like they were made of soggy old moor.

As I had a tiny bit of food
It made me in a very bad mood
I knew those pirates were real tough men
But I never want to see them ever again.

Noah Twine (8)
Milton Mount Primary School, Crawley

Senses Of Sea

As I stood on the pirate's deck
I saw the terrible captain whipping the screaming cabin boy
And when I looked up the sails blowing frantically
As I climbed the rough rigging
I felt myself shivering from the cold air
And eyes drilling into my back
As I went to tell that land was near
I heard their plots of stealing the governor's money
And suddenly a rumble of thunder and a clap of lightning
As I pulled at the rope
I smelt the sweat of other's bodies
And the smell of salty air.

Hollie Martin (9)
Milton Mount Primary School, Crawley

When I Was On The Pirate Ship

When I was on the pirate ship,
I could taste the stinging salt from the dirty sea
drying on my lips.
When I was on the pirate ship,
I could touch the treasure as it was glowing
on a sunny day.
When I was on the pirate ship,
I could hear the captain's loud singing, as he had
won the battle and stolen the treasure.
When I was on the pirate ship,
I could see the pirates fighting and it is still not
over yet, one hour later and it's still not over.
When I was on the pirate ship,
I smelt the blood of the pirates' flesh after a battle.

Stuart Beed
Milton Mount Primary School, Crawley

Scary Pirates

As I was doing some jobs for the captain
I smelt some horrible biscuits left with maggots and smelly legs
chopped off pirates
I saw desperate creatures after a dreadful battle, another ship
approaching the island
I tasted salt spray dried on lips and the stench on the pirates' clothes
I heard the pirates singing and cracking jokes and seagulls
screaming in the air
I touched the rusty old anchor chain and the rough wood of the deck.

Stewart Feasby (8)
Milton Mount Primary School, Crawley

On A Pirate Ship

I saw exhausted bodies of pirates
I saw desperate creatures approaching me
I saw blood-sodden men fighting a battle.

I heard the eerie sound of men howling
I heard the raging seas crashing the ship
I heard the swords clanging from a bloody battle.

I smelt the lovely smell of biscuits
I smelt the disgusting smell of blood dripping
I smelt the smell of the men's sweat.

I tasted the excitement of approaching land
I tasted the fear deep inside me
I tasted the biscuits with disgusting mite droppings inside.

I felt the splintering capstan that I moved
I felt the water of the sea while it was tossing the boat
I felt the fear of the unknown.

Naseem Bouchhar (8)
Milton Mount Primary School, Crawley

Pirate Poem

If I was a pirate's cabin girl
I would touch the rough tiller after I climbed the rigging.

If I was a pirate's cabin girl
I would taste the disgusting worms in the biscuits.

If I was a pirate's cabin girl
I would breathe the sea's salty air.

If I was a pirate's cabin girl
I would gaze at the everlasting sea
And wonder what it was like to find an island.

If I was a pirate's cabin girl
I would dream of having all the money that I could find all to myself.

Bethany Gray (8)
Milton Mount Primary School, Crawley

Pirates' Poem

When I jump on the pirates' ship
I taste the salty spray on my lips
I taste the bugs in the biscuits.

When I jump on the pirates' ship
I touch the hard rough rope covered in seaweed.

When I jump on the pirates' ship
I feel the ship is going to flip over and I shall die
I feel horrified there will be a battle soon.

When I jump on the pirates' ship
I see all the men fighting
I see a ship on the horizon
I hear blowing winds cracking the ship.

When I jump on the pirates' ship
I smell the horrible stench from the food
I smell the captain's skin.

Billy Towning (8)
Milton Mount Primary School, Crawley

Pirate Poem

If I was a cabin boy
I would touch the heavy rusty cannons that protect the old ship.

If I was a cabin boy
I would taste rock-hard bitter biscuit and offer some to
the captain's parrot.

If I was a cabin boy
I would breathe in the smell of a filthy pirate sweating in the sun.

If I was a cabin boy
I would gaze at the dazzling sea sparkling.

If I was a cabin boy
I would dream about being a captain in charge.

Theo Ray (8)
Milton Mount Primary School, Crawley

Pirate Poem

If I was a pirate's navigator
I would touch the spine chilling beard of the black hearted
Captain Red Kite.

If I was a pirate's navigator
I would taste the biscuits with wriggly weevils inside.

If I was a pirate's navigator
I would breathe the alcoholic stench of tasty grog.

If I was a pirate's navigator
I would dream of what we will find during our next frightful adventure.
I would gaze at the terrifying sight of a fellow pirate walking
the soaked plank.

Jonathan Comber (8)
Milton Mount Primary School, Crawley

Pirate Poem

If I was a member of the crew
I would touch the glistening, well-earned treasure from Heaven
in the battered sea chest.

If I was a member of the crew
I would taste a single salty drop from the world's most
monstrous ocean.

If I was a member of the crew
I would breathe in the high-pitched whistling wind surrounding me
With the whirls holding me tightly.

If I was a member of the crew
I would gaze at forks of fatal lightning with rumbling thunder
in the background.

If I was a member of the crew
I would dream of oceans fashioned with glorious treasure
And to be the richest living being to ever touch the Earth.

Max Pollock (8)
Milton Mount Primary School, Crawley

Pirate Poem

If I were a cabin girl
I would touch the razor-sharp beak of the emerald-green parrot.

If I were a cabin girl
I would taste the salty grog when the crew were asleep.

If I were a cabin girl
I would breathe in the smell of the burnt cooking and the extremely
salty sea.

If I were a cabin girl
I would dream of having the whole boat to myself
And all the treasure in the world.

Amy Young (9)
Milton Mount Primary School, Crawley

Henry Munday, Child Criminal

I am winter, when it's raining and lightning.
I am chickenpox and nobody wants to look at me.
I am a gigantic smock which has been ripped.
I am an old brick building, disgusting inside.
I am four days hard labour.
I am Henry Munday.

Luis Cousillas (9)
Milton Mount Primary School, Crawley

Henry Munday, The Child Criminal

I am winter when it is cold and foggy
I am a smelly old house which no one wants to live in
I am a piece of bread which is hard and mouldy that no one wants to eat
I am a shirt which is smelly and wet that no one wants to wear
I am a boil that is hard, red and full of puss
I am four days hard labour and whipped
I am Henry Munday.

Kobe Rice (9)
Milton Mount Primary School, Crawley

Henry Munday, A Child Criminal

I am the winter when it is freezing, gloomy and dark
I am a cold ancient workhouse that no one has entered for years
I am a sock that smells like cheese and that no one wants to wear
I am the plague that no one wants to come near
I am a battered and bruised banana that no one wants to eat
I am four days hard labour and whipped
I am Henry Munday.

Brooke Webb (10)
Milton Mount Primary School, Crawley

Henry Munday, The Child Criminal

I am winter in its deepest misery
I am salmonella which is highly contagious
I am a filthy, foul, grimy shoe that no one would want to wear
I am a battered, bitter, unsatisfying Brussels sprout that no one
could possibly eat
I am a craggy tarnished building that no one enters
I am a rusty pair of pliers that are used to pull teeth out
I am four days hard labour and whipped
I am Henry Munday.

John Ward (10)
Milton Mount Primary School, Crawley

Henry Munday, The Child Criminal

I am autumn when dead dull leaves fall to the ground
I am trousers which are ripped and rugged
I am a boil which is painful, revolting and full of puss
I am bread which is mouldy and rotten
I am the workhouse which is cramped and dirty
I am four days hard labour
I am Henry Munday.

Antonia Davis (10)
Milton Mount Primary School, Crawley

Henry Munday, The Child Criminal

I am cold and frozen with crushing leaves covering me
I am big horrible spots that no one wants to touch
I am a rugged old shoe with big holes, useless to wear
I am fourteen pints of strong sour ale, no one wants to drink
I am a rusty old building no one wants to enter
I am four days hard labour and whipped
I am Henry Munday.

Tommy May (9)
Milton Mount Primary School, Crawley

Henry Munday, The Child Criminal

I am winter when it's cold, dark and wet
I am a crooked, cramped, damp building that no one wants to live in
I am an old, stale, mouldy slice of bread which no one wants to eat
I am a dirty, old, tatty shoe which no one wants to wear
I am an oozing plague which no one wants to catch
I am four days hard labour and whipped
I am Henry Munday.

Alice Lloyd (9)
Milton Mount Primary School, Crawley

Henry Munday, The Child Criminal

I am winter, horrible gloomy weather when you wouldn't want to live on the streets
I am a prison, forbidding, smelly and gloomy
I am a smelly old sock which has been trampled on in the streets
I am a banana, tasteless and black
I am a large boil weeping out puss
I am four days hard labour and whipped
I am Henry Munday.

Eva Monoghan Moore (9)
Milton Mount Primary School, Crawley

Henry Munday, The Child Criminal

I am winter when it is snowing
I am a chickenpox which is smelly and disgusting
I am an old castle broken and empty
I am a cauliflower horrible and mouldy
I am a suit which is worn and ragged
I am four days hard labour and whipped
I am Henry Munday.

Rahel Miah (10)
Milton Mount Primary School, Crawley

Henry Munday, The Child Criminal

I am November when it's foggy and dark
I am a workhouse which is crooked and old
I am a crumb which is hard to see
I am a sock which is old and mouldy
I am scarlet fever which is horrible and nobody wants to catch me
I am four days hard labour and whipped
I am Henry Munday.

Jack Chappell (9)
Milton Mount Primary School, Crawley

Henry Munday, The Child Criminal

I am winter when it is cold and foggy
I am a painful large boil which no one wants to see
I am an old ragged sock which no one wants to wear
I am a piece of stale bread that no one wants to swallow
I am a dark gloomy building that no one wants to enter
I am four days hard labour and whipped
I am Henry Munday.

Ellie Fisher (9)
Milton Mount Primary School, Crawley

Henry Munday, Child Criminal

I am winter when it is very cold and wet
I am a painful boil full of puss that no one wants to see
I am a dirty, smelly and wet sock that no one wants to wear
I am a piece of fruit that has been in the gutter
I am a building that is very ancient and haunted
I am four days hard labour
I am Henry Munday.

Ella Marsh (9)
Milton Mount Primary School, Crawley

Pirate Poem

As I stood on the pirate ship's deck
I saw the horizon that had other pirates racing to try and get there first
I saw the treasure chest and the shipmates digging so they could
beat them.

As I stood on the pirate ship's deck
I heard the sea splashing against the ship
I heard the wind lashing the sails of the ship.

As I stood on the pirate ship's deck
I could smell the stinky rancid smell of the shipmates
And the smelly salty ocean.

As I stood on the pirate ship's deck
I touched the mouldy green water that was trickling down the ship
And the touch of the freezing cold sea.

As I stood on the pirate ship's deck
I tasted the spraying water on my tongue
I could taste the weevils in the powdery biscuits.

Joshua Benham (8)
Milton Mount Primary School, Crawley

Rain

It was a rainy winter's afternoon and everything was still.
Me and my brothers were as bored as the clouds looked
As they sulked high above us.
The rain swirled and danced
When it got caught by the wind,
Like the droplets were trying to escape
From the wild game of 'it' going on in the sky.
As it sparkled in the sunlight, we looked up in hope
That it may stop, but then the clouds swallowed up the sun
And we stared glumly through the window
As people in waterproof coats
Hurried home to warm up in front of the fire.
But my brothers raced wildly round the house
And John (he's the oldest) knocked over Mother's best vase.
She screamed at them to go away (but that's nothing new!)

I sighed and turned away,
My boredom was overwhelming me,
'Teatime,' Mother called and I trudged in to the kitchen,
I don't think I ever felt worse.
Till Mother dished up tea.
It was sludgy grey and it was as dark and damp as the sky.
'I am not eating that,' I told her
Before returning to the window.
It felt like I had plunged into a never-ending darkness,
A deep, dark hole of rain.
But then *it stopped!*
I ran in to the garden, it felt fresh and clean.
Well, I can play outside now,
Finally!

Vicky Ward (9)
Rudgwick Primary School, Horsham

Child's Disaster

Little child run along, don't look back or everything will go wrong
Run along child into the light, to get away from the darkness of night.
Oh innocent child what have you done?
Precious child get away from his gun
he may be your neighbour, friend or foe
Run, run, run, hurry up, go.

Poor little child I mourn for you on the floor
I asked you to run, nothing more
How could you know he could have killed
Without you my life isn't fulfilled.

I sip my cup of tea knowing you're not with me
I laughed at the TV, something was funny but you're not with me.

I go to sleep reaching high to grab your hand
And you show me your enchanting land
I still can't move now that you're gone
People give me sympathy, I don't want any
I want you back for good, I wish you would.

Yakira Traub (11)
St Andrew's CE Primary School, Hove

The Sea

The sea awoke in the morning,
The fish filled with glee.
Turtles flying peacefully parting the crystal clear ocean
It's a flowing paradise, nothing more, all is well
Until, until the black rocks of doom approach . . .
The waves crashing like boulders thrown into the water!
The sea now roaring in fear, rainbow-coloured coral
Turns into dark skeletons, all is dark in the ocean.

Elliot Meeten (11)
St Andrew's CE Primary School, Hove

Summer To Autumn, Winter To Spring

Summer sun, warm and happy, full of life
All the trees as green as grass
Everyone is out and about full with summer joy.

Winter is bitter, hardly anyone out
But winter can be happy too with one thing, Christmas
Sadly, it is just too cold to be like summer.

Summer getting colder and we have to go back to school
Summer is drawing closer to its end and the trees are going brown
Autumn is just around the corner.

Winter is going green and flowers popping out
The animals are waking up from winter just about
Everyone about pops their heads out of their houses.

Summer to autumn, winter to spring.

Gabrielle Rickman (11)
St Andrew's CE Primary School, Hove

Snow

A wisp of imagination falls from the sky
It sits on a comfy chair of grass
A white blanket of feathers covers the sheep
The snow it hurts their teeth like glass.

Snowmen large, snowmen small
They are different like us all
Wrapped up children everywhere
Throwing snowballs in the air.

Whiteness, whiteness everywhere
Till it turns all grey
It gets warmer overnight
It's gone by the next day.

Tom O'Donnell (10)
St Andrew's CE Primary School, Hove

Snow

White as a dove, the snow glistens and sparkles
Snowflakes elegantly dance in the vivid sunset,
The sea's waters are clear and still.

Night falls and the moon awakes from a deep sleep,
Jack Frost sprinkles his silver dust over the frozen town,
The town wakes up to a sheet of sugar.

Ice like a frozen diamond,
Tree branches are heavily laden with crumbly snow,
Dazzling ice fairies play in the tops of trees,
Children throwing snowballs to and fro.

Fraction by fraction the snow gradually fades away
But all is still
As a strip of snow glistens in the moonlight.

Holly Phillips (11)
St Andrew's CE Primary School, Hove

I Spy With My Little Eye

I spy with my little eye something that flies in the sky
I spy a little fly it flies so high in the sky
I spy a little fly, I spy with my little eye
I spy with my little eye I spy on a little fly
That flies so high in the sky
I spy with my little eye something that flies in the sky.

Bessie Phiri (11)
St Andrew's CE Primary School, Hove

Heartbeats Of Thought

It was dark, but I could hear the nurses
Monitoring my heartbeat and uttering curses.
Sluggish thoughts crawled into my head
As I tried to recall what was said.
'You will die ten years from now,
By plunging off the mountain.
And death will pour upon you
Like a black fountain.'

The first day we met was in the rain
In the midst of an animal rights campaign.
Our vegetarian hearts were entwined
The deepest true love anyone could find.
It was fantastic! How could anything go wrong?
Our shared love for animals was far too strong.

But before long, the prophecy was told
And her love for me went cold.
Two weeks later she married a prince
And from that day on, she always ate mince.
So that was it, all over,
I climbed the white cliffs of Dover.
All I could think of was my sweet Shirley,
So I jumped ten years too early.

The prophecy was right after all,
Ten years in a coma, now I'm the fool.
And now . . . I'm slipping . . . from life
And not one . . . soulmate . . . or wife.
My heart . . . now ceases . . . to beat
All . . .. I'll be now . . . is a lump . . . of meat.

Eden Townend (10)
St Andrew's CE Primary School, Hove

Six Wives

King Henry had six fine wives
But he wasn't pleased, so he took two to knives
And all for the sake of a scrimpy son
So he could carry the crown along.

His first wife was sweet Catherine
Who in fact nearly bagged almighty Queen
But in amongst it all she was dumped for the newest scene . . .
Queen Anne Boleyn took to his heart
But her odd set of fingers drew them apart
We think there might have been a snitch
For she was said to be a witch.

His third fine wife was Jane Seymour
Who Henry loved and she bore . . .
A strong and healthy son
But sadly when all is done she falls dead upon the floor.

Anne of Cleves was set for divorce
Because she was seen to resemble a horse
Alas, we have to move on
To see if he can get another son.

Catherine Howard was next in line
To have her share of blood-red wine
And in this I tell no lie
She was also set to die.

Katherine Parr was the final one
Who never did quite bare a son
Henry must have died in vain
For all the deaths he was to blame.

Josie Kemp (11)
St Andrew's CE Primary School, Hove

Summer Is A Never-Ending Wonder

The bright fresh morning opens its sleepy eyes
Fields and fields of luscious green, green grass
The clouds dance and play in the humid atmosphere
The summer ocean is a tropical paradise

Delicious creamy ice cream drips down the girls
In the boiling heat
Strawberries glisten, mangoes sing
And passion fruit sleeps all juicy and ready to eat.

Roses blossom with colours of love
The wind is warm and fresh and feels like Heaven
The magnificent sunset with all the colours of the rainbow
Beams on the pier.

Soon the dreamy sun starts to fade and waves goodbye
Clouds of mist cover the Earth
Suddenly it rains
A typical English summer
But summer is a never-ending wonder.

Bethany Swindells (11)
St Andrew's CE Primary School, Hove

Presents

It was Christmas Eve and everyone was quiet
Not even the dog made a sound.
I wished for one of my presents TNT,
My favourite drink,
My parents always got it for me.

The fire went out and the room went dark
Still nobody said anything they just groaned
My dad lit another fire, the room lit up
The dog began to bark and ran out the room
My dad followed but never came back.

I was in bed with my fingers crossed
My eyes were shining in the darkness
I heard my mum go downstairs
But she never came back up either
Now I was really scared.

I went downstairs in the morning
Waiting to open my presents
When I saw a shadow
It was not Mum or Dad's it was too thin
Then it lashed out and locked me in the living room
I rummaged through my presents
And found a box tagged TNT, I opened it
But what I first saw was a timer and the thing ran outside.

Tom Fookes (10)
St Andrew's CE Primary School, Hove

The Race

I'm speeding to the finish line
One hundred metres away
My legs are aching
I feel like stopping.

I'm speeding to the finish line
Seventy-five metres away
I hear the crowd shout, 'James,'
As I picture myself crossing the finish line.

I'm speeding to the finish line
Fifty metres away
'The trophy is mine,' I shouted loud,
'I will come first, second and third.'

I'm speeding to the finish line
Twenty-five metres away
Can I do it? Yes I can
Hip hip hooray.

I'm at the finish line
No metres away
I've crossed the line
I've won today.

Nia Healey Lewis (10)
St Andrew's CE Primary School, Hove

Snowstorm

A cold, blustery, freezing winter's morning
The wind picking up the force
Icicles huddle together keeping warm
The wind's howling cry deafens all the people.

Icicles frantically dancing in the wind
The wind's as strong as an elephant fighting for his child's life
Freezing bodies stumble around trying to find their long-lost homes
The ice covers all the people trying to hope for life.

People gaze up into the sky and see crystal-clear flakes
of iced glass snow
The hail is released as people frantically speed off
As the ferocious knuckles of doom hammer down on them
All hope is lost.

Icy whispers cry for help
As the wind's force smoothes
Shouts of joy as long-lost children are found
The wind grunts and will get revenge soon.

Georgina Cairns (10)
St Andrew's CE Primary School, Hove

Buddy

I'm a buddy and that's all right
I feel unhappy when I see friendships break up
Children fighting, arguing and shouting
That's disappointing.

I'm a buddy and it's enjoyable
I feel sad when I see bullying
Children name-calling, punching and kicking
That's upsetting.

I'm a buddy and it's all right
I feel pleased when I see friendships back together
Children talking, playing and joining buddy games
That's satisfactory.

I'm a buddy and it's enjoyable
I feel glad when I see less bullying
Children talking, playing and joining buddy games
That's brilliant.

Josh Freed (11)
St Andrew's CE Primary School, Hove

Houston, We Have A Problem

Saturn 5 roaring on the launch pad
A fiery white monster screaming into space
Sparks of excitement flying inside
The moon is nearing on this wonderful ride.

Bang! Apollo 13 is out of control
Evil black smoke rises from the hole,
'Houston, we have a problem,'
A long lonely way from NASA's emblem.

Apollo 13 passes by the moon
So nearly there, but gone too soon
Left in the small, dark, cold, thin air
Earth is a distant dream that I must dare.

Tearing through the cloudy atmosphere
Heart pounding, my breath is short with fear
Apollo 13 may not survive
A fireball screaming into the blue sea
The warm sun welcomes and I am free.

Sammy Martin (10)
St Andrew's CE Primary School, Hove

The Sea

The sea glistens in the moonlight
While the fish swim elegantly
Through the crystal clear coral reef
And the eels slither through the slippery seaweed.

There are many strange creatures in the ocean
Like sharks, whales and pretty pink fish
The ugly catfish to the pretty clown fish
And the manta ray that glides.

In the very, very, very deep depths
Creatures don't hunt
They feed; anything that dies is not wasted . . .

While on the surface
Where children play
Lie some predators
Hunting for their prey.

Max Gardiner (10)
St Andrew's CE Primary School, Hove

The Angry Sea

Sometimes she's nice, mostly she's not
The fierce sea crushed the boat with its angry hands
It pulled the men into its deadly mouth
Then the bones of the men floated up from the darkness
Blood all around them and you can smell it for miles.

The sea inky-blue waters crash on the pier legs
The sea created an angry storm which dragged people out to sea
Angrily the sea threw stones up onto the pier
Gnashing its teeth, the sea tries to eat the rope of the pier.

The sea let a tidal wave go and it grabbed all of the stones
And pulled them out to sea
He was very happy because he had destroyed the city.

Declan Brewster (11)
St Andrew's CE Primary School, Hove

The Deadly Sea

The dull sea, *silence,*
With cries in the misty air
The vile bodies sinking to the bottom of the ocean.

The roaring thunder strikes
At the vicious waves
Smothering the lonely boat.

The pebbles cackling like a wicked witch
The sharks tearing the still *heavy* bodies
Which lie afloat on the deep dark ocean.

Like a roaring rhino, the thundering strikes again
The boat gets crushed into specks
By the angry thunder and the wild waves.

The sea *shouts* at the terrifying thunder
And *silence . . .*
The war has finished.

Thomas Egeler (10)
St Andrew's CE Primary School, Hove

The Transformation Of The Sea

The sea is sleeping like a tired child waiting to be woken
It is a massive blue coat that shimmers like a polished floor
The sailors were on the breathing sea, in a boat bobbing up and down
At that the sea awoke
The angry sea tosses the boat to the jagged cliffs
Like a boy playing with a ball
The boat meets the sea floor in pieces and in triumph
The sea swells like an angry crowd
And then the sea subsided
And it was calm again
The man on the moon shone his bright light onto the sea
And once again the sea is sleeping like a tired child waiting
to be woken.

Oscar Reed (11)
St Andrew's CE Primary School, Hove

Bloodthirsty Ocean

A small fishing boat rocked side to side that night
The sailors had gone mad with fear
I was cradling myself to sleep that night
The sea was as evil as midnight hags
The storm was near.

The small fishing boat went back and forth
The sailors trembled with horror
I was on the boat that night
The sea was pounding her fists on our small fishing boat
The storm was near.

The small fishing boat was dragged under by the waves
The sailors dived off and disappeared
I made the mistake too
The waves plunged daggers into my heart
The sea was a murderer
The storm was near.

The small fishing boat was gone
The sailors were drowned
I felt the sea smashing my leg against the jagged rock till it split in two
The sea was as brutal as a slaughterer
The storm was near.

Without the small fishing boat
Or the ill and mental sailors
I was left to die horrifyingly
The sea was ripping me in half
The storm was near.

The small fishing boat had left me behind a plank of wood
The sailors had left me behind a shirt
I tried to seize them
But the sea wrenched me back
And smashed my broken and bleeding head on the rocky cliff
The sea was punishing me
The storm was near.

There I lay, frozen and motionless
For my life was finished
Forever
The sea, the waves, the ocean were punishing, ripping brutal murderers
But the storm had vanished.

Hannah Potterton (11)
St Andrew's CE Primary School, Hove

The Sea Is Death

She has mixed emotions
Her waves stand tall and fierce, angry
The pebbles crunch as she tosses them up
Into the bad-tempered air
I smell death.

I feel her icy hand grip my neck
I shiver, I feel alone, I feel vulnerable
The boulders cry for help
As the waves gallop towards them
I hear death.

A boat is splattered onto the harbour beach
Frothing like a boiling cauldron
A crackle of lightning
Splits the sky in two
I see death.

The wind warns me with a ghostly whisper
I hear myself scream
As the sea creeps nearer like a soft kitten
I feel death.

Florence Norgate (11)
St Andrew's CE Primary School, Hove

Stormy Seas

Raging rain, wailing wind
The bad-tempered sea
Like a volcano erupting
The fearless sea
Snatched the pebbles
Off the beach
And flung them into the midnight sky.

The sea air smelt like death
Power of the sea
Flung the boat into the inky-blue night sky
Powerlessly she pulled the vulnerable boat to the underworld
The wind howled like a wolf calling.

Clashing, crashing
She ripped the old wooden boat to shreds
She took a monstrous bite out of the fisherman's boat
Then threw it onto the other boats
She roared like a lion.

The seagulls awaken, another day begins
She is as still as a millpond
She is resting peacefully
After a hard night's work.

Lucy Kirby (11)
St Andrew's CE Primary School, Hove

Oh The Ferocious Sea

Choking in the grey mist not knowing where to go
She smashes boats and people into tiny smithereens
Her mighty power whipped until sailors were no more
She tugged them into her murky underworld
She bellowed like an angry giant and cackled like an evil witch
Oh the ferocious sea.

Her broad figure smashed boats into tiny pieces
Fingers of pain and despair
Stab my lonely heart taking away my life
Now I am a spirit lying in the inky-black darkness
I hear the menacing screams above making me shiver,
making me scared
Oh the ferocious sea.

I hear the sounds from above haunting me
I miss my mum, I miss my dad
Her jet-black lair smells like salt, just salt
I feel sick, dizzy, terrified
Oh the ferocious sea.

Alice Grant (11)
St Andrew's CE Primary School, Hove

The Sea

I stood on my yacht
Helplessly
I watched the storm grow
As a thick shroud of clouds covered the moon

She was angry
Angry with me
The hungry sharks were like her hunting dogs
Snapping at the boat
For she is the sea
The ghostly wind whispered taunts of death
Lightning strikes as her waves danced to the rhythm of the thunder
Rage rippled through her as she slammed into the pier
Mercilessly she threw the groynes at the town
My town
Anger flooded through me
For she had caused the death of my family, my friends
But through my rage, deep inside me
I felt frightened
I tried to run but I was stuck on my boat

Alone, all alone
Left to die
I screamed
Suddenly the sea stopped
Retreated slowly
Very slowly
And I was safe.

Clarissa Standen (10)
St Andrew's CE Primary School, Hove

The Sea And Her Evil Ways

Her white anger froths out of her
Spurting in the acid air like sparks of raging fire
She coils her ice-cold body round me
Squeezing my throbbing heart like a python
Killing its prey.

Her dagger-like claws pierce into my soul
Filling me with darkness
Harassing me, she tosses my body up and down in the waves
Playing with me like I'm a rag doll.

I feel myself being thrown in the air
And crashing down on the sharp angry rocks
Seaweed hooks round my wounded legs
Then drags me like snakes across the cackling pebbles into the evil sea.

The waves scoop the sand up into the inky midnight sky
It falls back down on me like sharp needles
The smell of blood and flesh stains the air
From every victim the sea has killed.

I want to get out of here
I want to escape this cruel world
But somehow - somehow I know
That there will no longer be any tomorrow for me.

Ellie Homewood (11)
St Andrew's CE Primary School, Hove

The Dull Sea

The grey sky beckoned death
The smell of salt filled my nose
Fingers of death drag me into the inky darkness of the underworld
She gripped the boat and pulled it under to her watery lair.

The sea crashed into the pier
And clattered it over into murky water
The sea threw itself in the air
Like an angry giant going to war.

Pebbles clamber over each other
The waves like a volcano erupting
I feel darkness
Time's up
Run
Fall
Death
The dull sea
Gnashing its jaws
Coming for me!

Jessie Ward (10)
St Andrew's CE Primary School, Hove

Clouds Poem

The white clouds
Pollution's worst enemy
The red planet Mars
Mars
The red planet laughs
At the sun's best friend
Earth
The fierce sea
Roared and punched
At the sad boat
Smashing it
Side to side
The world
Full of life and joy
Skipping happily across
Like a boy
Who just got a picture
Of his white clouds.

William Walsh (11)
St Andrew's CE Primary School, Hove

The Menacing Sea

The sea
The menacing, ferocious sea
Carelessly she flings sleepy clutter
Scattering it along the terrified beach
She rears up and roars violently
Then
Comes back down
Whipping the salty polished rocks.

The waves march in unison
While the pebbles dance in the air
To the rhythm of the thunder
Her hands clasp around a helpless boat
Coiling round it
Pulling it into her murky underworld
For she is the sea
The menacing, ferocious sea.

Screaming, the pebbles give me warnings
Not to come near or she will capture my soul too
She will not spare anyone's life
For she is the sea
The menacing, ferocious sea.

But, it's too late
Her claws creep round my neck
She slowly pulls me in
Squeezing my neck tighter
Powerless, my lungs shrivel
My heart pounds
Why is she doing this?
Because she is the sea
The menacing, ferocious sea.

I squeal for help
I smell the bitter air filling my nostrils
I hear her hushing me, pulling me down
For she is the sea
The menacing, ferocious sea.

Hannah Corcoran (10)
St Andrew's CE Primary School, Hove

The Cruel, Strange Sea

The sea
The cruel, strange sea
Some days she is kind, some days she is not
Like a baby chuckling to itself, she giggles in her sleep
Silently gliding across the sleeping sea
The glowing moon stalks the ghostly town
Suddenly she awakes
Breaking through the quietness
Like a volcano erupting
Cackling with laughter, she tosses stones up in the sky
Then falling into the roaring mouth of the sea
She flings boats and terrified people into the midnight air.

The wailing wind whistles like a widow mourning
After her husband's death
Then a girl came
A lonely, vulnerable girl
Wandering up to the sea
The sea was angry, angry as a lion in a fight
Angry that she dare come that close to her
Guarding herself
Waves march in parallel lines like soldiers at war
She springs at her prey, spraying her,
Helping seaweed wrap around her like a shroud
Pulling her into the darkness of the deep blue underworld
Then lightning flashed, thunder crashed
Like a ferocious rhino
Wind cried then silence
The waves and sea stopped
She's asleep
Sound asleep, setting the girl free
The sea
The cruel, strange sea.

Katie Dinnage (10)
St Andrew's CE Primary School, Hove

The Sea At Midnight

Crashing, clashing
A bad-tempered storm
Raging rain
Wailing wind
The violent sea like a roaring lion
Trying to set free.

A blanket of black clouds
Gnashing jaws of a deadly shark
Tentacles that hooked on
Like a lock and key
She creeps up behind the sand
Then snatches it away
Down, down . . .
To the underworld.

She grabbed the pebbles
Teasing them
Then tossed them
Into the midnight air, death-like air.

The wind like a howling wolf
The dull sea
The vulnerable sea
Wizened, icy-cold fingers
Run down my spine
As I feel the cold, ghostly breeze.

Martha Borrow (11)
St Andrew's CE Primary School, Hove

The Evil Laugh

Bellowing as loud as a lion
The sea crashed into the docks
Back and forth it marched violently
With an evil laugh.

Ice-cold fingers ran down my back
I called out in desperation
To the sea
It gave me an evil laugh.

The murky water grabbed me
I was a vulnerable rag doll
Being played with by an aggressive child
She, with an evil laugh.

The whistling wind blew my hair
The black shroud of water
Covered me
With an evil laugh.

Wizened fingers grabbed my clothes
Grabbed my hair
Then let me go
No evil laugh?

Was it over?
The Earth stilled
In the distance, I heard
An evil laugh.

Ellie Barnham (11)
St Andrew's CE Primary School, Hove

Antarctica's Mystery

On the misty horizon the red ball of fire awakened
From her deep, deep sleep
Glistening upon the crystal, clear, icy waters
In the distance a flock of skuars ambled elegantly greeting
the morning sun
The wind was a soft and gentle melody whilst whirling and having fun.

The ocean flowed swiftly in the breeze with magical ease
Like a youngster's heart filled with joy
It was a gentle and serene baby being nurtured by its mother
In the distance a huddle of black fearsome wolves
Appeared and a blue sheet of sadness was a cover
At the speed of lightning, icebergs loomed almost reaching eternity.

Creaking and groaning like a hungry ogre, Antarctica had awakened
The deafening thunder bellowed like a roaring lion
Protecting its young and the Earth has just been shaken.

Lightning had arrived, striking the violent waves
As it threw its deadly tantrum into the howling and blustery winds
as it misbehaved
Silence, silence, not a word to be heard
But the corrupt and mysterious stillness of the world.

The rugged monster calmed itself down
As the snowflakes battled off the frost, they fell to the ground
They twirled gracefully in the mellow breeze
As the sparkling sunlight began to unfreeze
The mist bounced off the thumb-numbing ice.

On the horizon the sun fell, wept and waved goodbye
And hides behind the clouds for she is so shy
The moon had risen as it glistened upon the icy waters
For the shadow it cast began to seem shorter.

Amber Van Day (10)
St Andrew's CE Primary School, Hove

The Pack

Trees glistening with snow
The ground, one huge white duvet
Silence echoes around the forest
As they wait for spring to come again.

The silence is ripped apart by barks
As forty mastiffs
Lean in body
Chase after their prey.

A white rabbit
Sniffing for food
Runs when it hears the dogs
It runs as fast as it can.

Disaster strikes
As one mastiff falls over
Another falls over the first
They will not get up again.

The hunt carries on
Until they lose the rabbit
And the huntsman
Tired and angry
Leads his pack home.

Trees glistening with snow
The ground, one huge white duvet
Silence echoes around the forest
As they wait for spring to come again.

Veronica Zambon (11)
St Andrew's CE Primary School, Hove

The Storm

It came to be nightfall and all the men from their day's work
came home
As the fishermen were getting their boats in the harbour
The last boat came in and a father and a son were there
Then it started to rain over the sea a pitter-patter and that's
how it started.

Then the rain got harder and quicker
All of it sounded like drums, drums in the deep
The winds were twice the size of any ship
The fishermen just got inside but the great harbour wall
Did not seem so great when the waves hit them.

Thunder and lightning hit houses and buildings
It sounded like a blacksmith hitting iron and the soot
In the dark with a *bang, bang, bang, bang*
It was a great storm.

Then the clouds shifted and the sun reached out
And birds started to sing
All the people came out and started to celebrate
And that was the last storm, storm, storm
The last storm.

Louis Alexander (10)
St Andrew's CE Primary School, Hove

Premonition

It was late at night
I was dozing by the fire
Drifting to sleep under warm lamp light
Sipping at hot cocoa.

A knock on the door
I jumped and my cocoa spilt
My newspaper fell to the floor
Unread headlines screamed *beware!*

Down the dark hallway, growing in fright
My heart beat quicker as I reached for the handle
A sinister figure stepped out of the night
And something glinted by his side . . .

With a cry he drew a blade
And with one short snap
Everything began to fade
I fell to the floor and -

I was back in my seat
Back by the fire
All just a dream, my paper's neat
My cocoa's unspoilt, all was peaceful . . . I jumped -
There was a knock on the door . . .

Sam French (11)
St Andrew's CE Primary School, Hove

Winter

The air is crisp and cold
Summer now seems so old
Forget-me-not blue skies above
With clouds as white as a dove.

Memories of hot happy hours
Of birds and sun and flowers
Spending days by the sea and sand
With our buckets and spades in hand.

But winter winds blow near
And Christmas will soon be here
Blazing fires to warm dark nights
With carol singers and Christmas lights.

Crowds of shoppers rush to and fro
Hoping for some festive snow
Buying brightly-coloured Christmas ribbon
For the presents to be given.

Siobhan Stack-Maddox (11)
St Andrew's CE Primary School, Hove

Chuckle Bug

Squeezing like a giant pinch
A hand grabs at my guts
Oh no, run to the toilet
My class doesn't need to see my lunch.

My mum collected me from school
I went home and had a bath
Afterwards I switched on the telly
And Barry Chuckle made me laugh!

Rémi Lord (11)
St Andrew's CE Primary School, Hove

The Sea

The sea is like a torrent of darkness
Its waves are just like thunder striking its every move.

The sea is like a dark man in the river
It moves its way up to the end of the sea
The man has always wanted to get his revenge.

The sea is just like a dark moment of history
As the man reaches the end of the sea
In excitement he gets ready for revenge.

At last the sea man has got to the end
He says, 'At last, I have got to where I'm going to play my revenge!'

The sea is like a torrent of darkness
Its waves are just like thunder striking its every move.

Agbude Eseoghene (11)
St Andrew's CE Primary School, Hove

The Sun

The sun rises early in the morning
Lighting up the days
Waking people up from their sleep.

The sun warms people up
As they get out of the sea
Making them dry.

The sun watches the sausages sizzle
On the barbecue
And smiles at the children as they happily play.

The sun slowly closes her eyes
As she falls asleep
Ready to rise early in the morning.

Charlotte Ward (10)
St Andrew's CE Primary School, Hove

Fairies From Good To Evil

Their wings sparkle like the midnight moon
And their glistening tiaras shimmer
The reflection of magic in the air
Camouflages into the sorcerer's lake
Then darkness arrives
Into the minds of the innocent people
Their fireflies die away into the spooky night light
Will they survive or let them take over their souls?

Ashleigh Cosham (11)
St Andrew's CE Primary School, Hove

Open The Door

(Inspired by 'The Door' by Miroslav Holub)

Go and open the door
Maybe there's a black cat sitting quietly outside the door
Maybe there's a fluffy rabbit leaping like a joyful cat
Maybe there's a golden dog running like a cheetah
Maybe there's a chocolate volcano erupting in the mountains.

Matthew Clifford (8)
Saltdean CP School, Saltdean

The Open Door

(Inspired by 'The Door' by Miroslav Holub)

Go and open the door
Maybe the years have flown by and it's the year 3,000,000
Maybe there's a Mazda RX7 speeding down the zigzag road
Maybe there's a monster truck as big as the universe
Maybe there's a 100% dark chocolate swimming pool worth dying for.

Toby Corner (8)
Saltdean CP School, Saltdean

The Open Door

(Inspired by 'The Door' by Miroslav Holub)

Go and open the door
Maybe there is a friendly Dalek that is tidying all of the toys in the shop
Maybe there is a galloping horse like a flying unicorn
Maybe there are two leaping giants like a bouncy ball
Maybe there are two baby lions lying on the shimmering floor
Maybe there are laughing lions that are playing with toilet rolls.

Olivia Turner (9)
Saltdean CP School, Saltdean

The Open Door

(Inspired by 'The Door' by Miroslav Holub)

Go and open the door
Maybe there are five leaping lollies melting in the sizzling sun
Maybe there is a flipping frog doing headstands under
the midnight moon
Maybe there is a headless horseman doing the cha-cha
Maybe there is a jumping giant working at the Co-op
Maybe there is a sizzling sausage racing with a tiger.

Olivia Bowman (9)
Saltdean CP School, Saltdean

The Open Door

(Inspired by 'The Door' by Miroslav Holub)

Go and open the door
Maybe there is a beautiful snake
Maybe there is a great dragon walking down the road
like a colossal bear
Maybe there is a fountain
Maybe there is a brilliant cat.

Danielle Long (9)
Saltdean CP School, Saltdean

The Open Door

(Inspired by 'The Door' by Miroslav Holub)

Go and open the door
Maybe there's a glittering waterfall tumbling down the rocks
Maybe there's a stretched-out jungle that carries on forever and ever
Maybe there are mountains standing like stiff solid ice
Maybe there are shimmering zebras
Singing and dancing quickly around the great stone of life.

Alina Vincent (8)
Saltdean CP School, Saltdean

The Open Door

(Inspired by 'The Door' by Miroslav Holub)

Go and open the door
Maybe there are animals like bouncy balls jumping up at you
Maybe there's chocolate melting like the burning sun shining down onto the Earth
Maybe there are sweets piled like a tall tower on the ground
Maybe there's colourful balloons floating up in the sky.

Summer Tyrrell (8)
Saltdean CP School, Saltdean

The Open Door

(Inspired by 'The Door' by Miroslav Holub)

Go and open the door
Maybe outside there's a glossy ghost singing under the moon
Maybe there are laughing lollipops playing games and watching TV
Maybe there is a dancing dormouse playing the guitar
Maybe there is a sizzling sausage burning in a pan
Maybe there is a laughing lion doing the ironing.

Sophie Walker (9)
Saltdean CP School, Saltdean

The Open Door

(Inspired by 'The Door' by Miroslav Holub)

Go and open the door
Maybe there is a mathematical genius making up a way
for the number 3 to become 5
Maybe there is a flying carpet doing yoga with a chalky statue
Maybe there is a dancing lion who acts like he's a professional
Maybe there are leaping lollies going around a room in a circle
Maybe there is a talking dog playing poker with his dog friends.

Alexandra Black (9)
Saltdean CP School, Saltdean

The Open Door

(Inspired by 'The Door' by Miroslav Holub)

Go and open the door
Maybe outside there's a dancing dinosaur grooving the night away
Maybe there's a funny fish giggling through the day
Maybe there is a chocolate land melting in the sun
Maybe there's a large meerkat moving at the top of the hill
Maybe there's a glowing hand brightening up a darkened room.

Amy Perkins (9)
Saltdean CP School, Saltdean

The Open Door

(Inspired by 'The Door' by Miroslav Holub)

Go and open the door
Maybe outside there is a sly snake waving his tongue around
Maybe there is a funny fish splashing around the pond
Maybe there are two loud lollipops jumping about
Maybe there are three sizzling sausages being sizzled in a saucepan
Maybe there are spotty trees tickling another tree's toes.

Tegan Jackson (8)
Saltdean CP School, Saltdean

The Open Door

(Inspired by 'The Door' by Miroslav Holub)

Go and open the door
Maybe outside the luxurious chocolate river is crashing down
the rapids
Maybe there is a smiley dog running in a cheerful river
Maybe there are 1,000 dogs waiting outside
Maybe there is a unicorn who is shy and scared
Maybe there is a giant gingerbread house that I could live in.

Connie Savage (8)
Saltdean CP School, Saltdean

The Open Door

(Inspired by 'The Door' by Miroslav Holub)

Go and open the door
Maybe outside there is a smiling sunflower laughing sweetly at me
Maybe there are two kind kittens sharing their fish with the trees
Maybe there is a dozing dish sleeping with a spoon
Maybe there is a funny fairy trying to find her butterflies
Maybe there are ten tap-dancing teabags humming to the tango
Maybe there is only a gust of wind whistling at the window.

Shirley Marchant (8)
Saltdean CP School, Saltdean

The Open Door

(Inspired by 'The Door' by Miroslav Holub)

Go and open the door
Maybe outside there is a leaping cow jumping over the moon
Maybe there is a talking dog sitting on the wall in the sun
Maybe there is a friendly Dalek scaring some rabbits
Maybe there is a dancing dinosaur stamping his feet
Maybe there is a zooming zombie chasing my aunt.

Dane Lind (8)
Saltdean CP School, Saltdean

The Open Door

(Inspired by 'The Door' by Miroslav Holub)

Go and open the door
Maybe outside there is a spotty cow jumping over the moon
Maybe there is a horse dancing in a farmyard
Maybe there is a sleeping pig watching the TV
Maybe there is an army of socks who are shy and smelly
Maybe there is a gust of wind shaking the trees.

Jake Lind (8)
Saltdean CP School, Saltdean

The Open Door

(Inspired by 'The Door' by Miroslav Holub)

Go and open the door
Maybe outside there's a lion's mane like shining gold in the sunlight
Maybe there are two jumping giants jumping down the clifftop
Maybe there is a funny fish dancing in the dark like a dangerous diver
Maybe there is a scary singer flying a jet plane
Maybe there is a jumping cow jumping over the moon.

Oliver Turner (9)
Saltdean CP School, Saltdean

The Open Door

(Inspired by 'The Door' by Miroslav Holub)

Go and open the door
Maybe outside there is a family of robot dogs trying to find
a giant bone
Maybe there is a talking teabag chattering to his friends
Maybe there are some funny fish leaping around the water
making splashes
Maybe there are some spotty yellow trees swaying in the wind
Maybe there is a pouncing penguin laughing to himself.

Charlotte Cooke (9)
Saltdean CP School, Saltdean

The Open Door

(Inspired by 'The Door' by Miroslav Holub)

Go and open the door
Maybe outside there is a spotty yellow tree walking around
greeting people
Maybe there is a dizzy donkey as dizzy as running around in circles
for 1,000 years
Maybe there are not-so-enchanted fairies trying to magically cast
spells that don't work
Maybe there are five chilly chickens freezing and not minding at all
Maybe there are flying penguins like seagulls over the deep blue sea.

Vita Smith (8)
Saltdean CP School, Saltdean

The Open Door

(Inspired by 'The Door' by Miroslav Holub)

Go and open the door
Maybe outside there are flying pigs talking to pink trees
Maybe there are bouncy balls jumping way up high
Maybe there are talking teapots sizzling like sausages
Maybe there are enormous worms playing games and watching TV
Maybe there's a land of chocolate with no dentists.

Suzannah Gilburt (8)
Saltdean CP School, Saltdean

The Open Door

(Inspired by 'The Door' by Miroslav Holub)

Go and open the door
Maybe there's a shimmering waterfall rushing through the rocks
Maybe there's space as far as the eye can see
Maybe there's a dragon expelling scorching fire like a volcano
Maybe there's a rhino having a mega-battle against a great elephant.

Elizabeth Golding (8)
Saltdean CP School, Saltdean

The Open Door

(Inspired by 'The Door' by Miroslav Holub)

Go and open the door
Maybe there's a pretty waterfall like a beautiful sheet of blue
Maybe there's a magnificent chocolate cake for me to share with you
Maybe there's a tiny kitten with eyes like a cluster of stars
Maybe there's a bunch of roses and a golden racing car
Maybe there's an enchanted wood with a tree as high as the sky
Maybe there's a pair of wings and when I wear them I can fly
Maybe there's a dazzling unicorn
Maybe a rhinoceros with a sharp and pointy horn
Maybe there's a land of sweets and when you eat some no one minds
Maybe there's an angel who is really kind.

Lucy Rodgers (8)
Saltdean CP School, Saltdean

The Open Door

(Inspired by 'The Door' by Miroslav Holub)

Go and open the door
Maybe outside there is an amazing time machine travelling
at the speed of light
Maybe there are two laughing lions telling jokes to each other
on the sandy beach
Maybe there is a dozing dog curled up in the shiny sun
Maybe there is a speedy tortoise racing a cheating cheetah across
the desert
Maybe there are five tango teabags dancing the salsa
Just go and open the door.

Peter Sowerby (8)
Saltdean CP School, Saltdean

The Open Door

(Inspired by 'The Door' by Miroslav Holub)

Go and open the door
Maybe there's a beautiful fish swimming in the lovely sea
Maybe there's a luscious chocolate pool calling my name
Maybe there's a sun shining like the moon
Maybe there's a red Ferrari waiting for me.

Sidney Mohns (9)
Saltdean CP School, Saltdean

Open The Door

(Inspired by 'The Door' by Miroslav Holub)

Go and open the door
Maybe there's a penguin waddling like a duck
Maybe there's a horse running through the long green field
Maybe there's a tortoise swimming through the moving water
Maybe there's a waterfall twinkling through the bumpy rocks
Maybe there's a dragon flying in the blue sky
Maybe there's a melting chocolate pool like a golden stone.

Mia Ross (8)
Saltdean CP School, Saltdean

The Open Door

(Inspired by 'The Door' by Miroslav Holub)

Go and open the door
Maybe there is a gigantic football ground
Maybe there is a big fish bowl and with sparkling water
Maybe there is a shimmering swimming pool like a glass
of shining water
Maybe there is a chocolate bar as big as a massive volcano.

Connor Lawday (9)
Saltdean CP School, Saltdean

The Open Door

(Inspired by 'The Door' by Miroslav Holub)

Go and open the door
Maybe there's a mouth-watering chocolate fountain
Making me tempted to pop a marshmallow in and eat it
Maybe there's a horse shimmering like a beautiful sunset
Maybe there's an adorable puppy leaping with all four paws
off the ground
Maybe there's a chocolate swimming pool that you can drink
and it never runs out.

Liliana Salih-Miller (8)
Saltdean CP School, Saltdean

The Open Door

(Inspired by 'The Door' by Miroslav Holub)

Go and open the door
Maybe there's a black Bugatti waiting dismally like the gloomy
midnight sky
Maybe there's a white chocolate waterfall that's waiting
to be discovered
Maybe there's a rare computer with every programme on its hard drive
Maybe there's a land of crisps waiting to be consumed.

Thomas Milne (9)
Saltdean CP School, Saltdean

The Open Door

(Inspired by 'The Door' by Miroslav Holub)

Go and open the door
Maybe outside the scaly green dragon's scales shine like gold
Maybe there's a gold Ferrari zooming down the wobbly road
Maybe there is a tortoise running to his home in Africa
Maybe there is a shy and smiley face staring at you.

Daniel Fernell (8)
Saltdean CP School, Saltdean

The Magnificent Dolphin

My dolphin leaps like a rocket flying to the heavens
He is grey like an elephant lumbering across the plains
He is graceful like the prince of the sea
He sweeps through the sea like a quiet lawnmower
A rescuer like a lifeguard waiting to be called to the sea
He clicks like a radar sending a secret message
He resembles a moonlight dancer
I will honour you with all my life.

Evan Ridley (8)
Saltdean CP School, Saltdean

Gently

Gently the shivering snow falls from the sky
Gently a red flower shoots up higher and higher
Gently a golden horse trots around with a big sigh
Gently the tall tree sways from side to side
Gentle is the moonlight but gentlest of all
Is a silent wall about to fall.

Bethany Leak (9)
Saltdean CP School, Saltdean

Gently

Gently the gazelle gallops through the grass
Gently the tortoise strides into the jungle
Gently the cheetah sprints to his prey
Gently the cat jumps carefully onto a lap
Gentle as a feather dropping from the sky
Gentlest of all is the little puppy playing with his ball.

Guy Bolton (9)
Saltdean CP School, Saltdean

The Magnificent Snake

My snake is slithery like a slimy toad that has lost its legs
His tail is like a poisonous stick
His face is like a sharp needle
His eyes are like tumbling spreading mountains
He resembles grass that always stays green
I will treasure you like a piece of gold.

Ethan Walker (8)
Saltdean CP School, Saltdean

Loudly

Loudly the volcano releases its red-hot lava
Loudly the tsunami crashes against the town
Loudly the mammoth's trunk calls to its family
Loudly the lion's roar shouts for help
Loud is the sea crashing against the rocks
But the loudest of all is an earthquake coming towards us.

Jack Buckingham (9)
Saltdean CP School, Saltdean

Gently

Gently the grass sways on a hot sunny day
Gently the eagle flies to catch its prey
Gently the old man's writing flows
Gently the tide comes in
But gentlest of all is the softest feather tumbling down.

Oskar Jones (8)
Saltdean CP School, Saltdean

The Mirror

'Don't you dare go near my new mirror while I'm asleep,' said my mum
But I did
It was so beautiful, surrounded by red rubies gleaming in the sun
I could not resist, I had to touch it
I stood for a moment . . . then *crash!*
It smashed into little pieces smothering the floor
All that was left was the outer rim of rubies and some of them
had fallen out.

'What was that noise dear?'
'The cat,' I said.
I heard footsteps coming from upstairs, I was shaking with fear.
'How's the cat dear?'
'All right now,' I said.
'What is that?'
'I don't know.'
I was in for it now
I knew it . . .

Stella O'Neil (8)
Saltdean CP School, Saltdean

Animals

A squawking parrot and barking dogs
Slippery snakes, funny frogs
Mysterious monkeys and cute cats
Hamsters, gerbils and running rats.

Beautiful butterflies, busy bees
Lobsters and sharks who rule the seas
Prickly porcupines, small snails
Fish, crabs and whopping great whales!

Terrific turtles and outstanding owls
Lazy lizards and guinea fowls
Quacking ducks and smiling stoats
Huge horses and billy goats.

Lea Donovan (8)
Saltdean CP School, Saltdean

Gently

Gently the cute kitten slept on the bouncy bed
Gently the slow tortoise crawled away
Gently the fluffy puppy dug a big hole
Gently the little bunny jumped around
Gentle is the feather
But gentlest of all is the soft tiny sparrow that hops from the wall.

Karni Jury (9)
Saltdean CP School, Saltdean

Why?

Why do people die?
Why am I 10?
Why was I born?

Why? Why? Why?

Why am I living?
Why do I have to go to school?
Why are we on this planet?

Because, because, because . . .

People die to keep the population down!
I am 10 because I have lived for 10 years!
I was born because I was.

Because, because, because . . .

I live because I am not dead,
I go to school for education,
We are on this planet because it has all the things we need.

Frazer Earl (10)
West Park CE Middle School, Worthing

Witches

There was once this witch who was ugly but mean
She one turned a dragon from purple to green
She was very lazy and had a mad laugh
For 5,000 years she'd never had a bath!

Now I must warn you witches are freaky and smelly
She thinks she's pretty, but she's got a big fat belly
Now you know everything about witches
They are cruel and evil and have lots of stitches!

So as you know everything about witches
You know they like spells
They're ugly and have weird twitches
So now you probably think evil witches are weird
Just wait and see her twelve inch beard.

Jessica Battell (9)
West Park CE Middle School, Worthing

Football

Football is fab
Football is cool
Football can be more than a ball
Football can be fun
Football is wicked
Overall football is cool.

Sophie Bishop (9)
West Park CE Middle School, Worthing

Snow Is

Snow is . . .
A miracle, a dream, snow is here
Snow is like a field of dreams on my lawn
Snow means joy and fun
Snow is as sticky as honey
Snow is as juicy as a cucumber
Snow is fluffy like candyfloss
Snow is shiny like silver on the road
Snow is funny
Snow thaws
Snow is gentle
Snow is raw
Snow is soft and slushy
Snow is *great!*
I like snow, do you?

Ryan Sopp & Kristian Binns (9)
West Park CE Middle School, Worthing

Snowflakes

Snowflakes are like little moons
Snowflakes dance to the wind's tunes
Snowflakes fall on top of cars
Snowflakes fall like they're from Mars
Snowflakes shine and shimmer
Snowflakes glow and glitter
Snowflakes are luminous in the moonlight
Snowflakes melt in the night's light
Snowflakes, snowflakes, snowflakes!

Abigail Else (9)
West Park CE Middle School, Worthing

Sky

I love the sun in the sky
All warm on my face
I like the background of the blue
With a shimmer of white cotton balls

I love the shine of a new moon
The darkness of the sky
With twinkles of stars
That light up as I walk on by

The dark clouds roam like stampeding cattle
With the pitter-patter of rain or a clash of thunder
Maybe the soft flutter of snowflakes
Falling on my face

Whatever the weather
Whatever the day
I love the sunshine
In every way.

Joshua Borgars (8)
West Park CE Middle School, Worthing

Snowman

When you build a snowman at night
The snow looks like it's glowing
A soft fat tummy
A black beady mouth
Small currant eyes
An orange carrot nose
A grey checked hat
A blue spotty scarf
Brown stick arms
I am a snowman
You can only build me
If you have frosty wishes.

Katherine Germaine & Mia Walton (9)
West Park CE Middle School, Worthing

Snakes - I Wonder If They Have Brakes?

Long and scaly with evil eerie grins
Their eyes glint with a thousand sins.
Their fangs hang down like stalagmites,
Its venom will give you more than a fright.

Snakes,
I wonder if they have brakes?

Small, cute and furry, one mouse is for lunch,
Although, it's far better to have a bunch.
Sometimes when they're looking for a treat,
They can even manage a parakeet.

Snakes,
I wonder if they have brakes?

Slithering around the trunks of trees,
Elegant and beautiful, they live as they please.
Coiled tight as a bow spring, they await their prey,
Patience is a virtue, it could take all day.

Snakes,
I don't think they have brakes!

Taylor McGuire (10)
West Park CE Middle School, Worthing

What Is Red?

Red is blood trickling down your knee
Red is the colour of the bright red crab
Red is the colour of somebody mad
Red is the colour of somebody's cheeks
Red is the witch's frog potion
Red is the colour of somebody's emotion.

Samuel Empson (9)
West Park CE Middle School, Worthing

Snow

Snow is like little crystals falling down from the sky to the big
white-covered floor
Snow means lots of snowball fights
Snow makes me cold, it makes my hands tremble with coldness
When come in I have a hot chocolate drink that makes my hands
feel as warm as love.

Iyesha Adebisi (8)
West Park CE Middle School, Worthing

Hawks

The hawks soar above the ground
Like a group of kites gliding amongst the clouds
Suddenly one spots her prey hopping out of its burrow
Like a dart she seeks her target
Frozen for a second then regaining its strength it scurries off
Better luck next time!

Elise Price (9)
West Park CE Middle School, Worthing

Friend

F riends stick together always
R eliable
I n touch
E ndlessly fun
N ever not there
D elightful.

Tabbie Earl (9)
West Park CE Middle School, Worthing

My Day

The golden sand goes on forever, as far as the eye can see
My filly feels as free as the wind that whispers through my hair
I hold her reins lightly, letting her canter in the surf
Feeling the cool droplets splashing my bare feet
I feel the warmth of the golden sun caressing my face like soft kisses
I think, *what a glorious day, I wish it would never end*
I am as one with my horse, she is as one with me, we are one
Her coat glistens with spume, each droplet holding a rainbow
Her breath is as calm as the summer breeze, the palms sway slowly
in a gentle zephyr
The sound of the surf running up the beach is in perfect time
with her hoof-beats
Her eyes reflect the sea like mirrors
What a lovely day, this is my day
What a perfect day!

Rebecca Hoibak (9)
West Park CE Middle School, Worthing

Tigor

There she walks in the forest as silent as a mouse
With her glassy eyes she prowls around
Black and orange stripes which keep her camouflaged
In the forest she prowls.

Then in front of her is a pool of water
She jumps into the middle of the pool
And swims to the other side
There in front of her is a cave
And inside are her cubs!

Hannah Boyle (10)
West Park CE Middle School, Worthing

Anger

Anger is like a rocket ready to *blast!*
Anger is like a volcano about to *explode!*
Anger is thunder *booming* in the air!
Anger is lightning *crackling* in my head!
Anger is a bully ready to fight
Anger is a feeling no one wants to have
Anger is something sometimes you just can't control
Anger is my face when it goes red.

Sam Cummings (9)
West Park CE Middle School, Worthing

Snow

Snow, snow, you are so cold
Snow, snow, you are cold as can be
Snow, snow, you fall from the sky
Snow, snow, you are as happy as can be
Snow, snow, you can make snowballs
That are white as can be.

Lewis Amesbury-Fuller (9)
West Park CE Middle School, Worthing

There Was A Man Called Mu

There was a man called Mu
He had the nasty flu
He ate lamb
With a lump of jam
Then he needed the loo!

Tristan Martin (9)
West Park CE Middle School, Worthing

Hate

H ate is when you feel bad and don't like someone
A lso hate makes you feel like you want to burst
T here's hate that turns into love and love that turns into hate
E veryone can hate and want to hurt someone else
Sometimes hate leaves if you just say *sorry!*

Lauren Bromley (10)
West Park CE Middle School, Worthing

The Magic Forest

Flowers, butterflies, here and there
Left, right, front, back, everywhere.

Hop, hop, over there
Rabbits hopping behind the bushes.

Hang on a minute, what do I see
Is that a goblin behind the tree?

Zoom, zoom, here and there
Pixies zooming around the forest.

I hear footsteps behind me
I'm turning around very swiftly
It's a baby deer running away from me.

Tiffany Watson (9)
West Park CE Middle School, Worthing

Nula

N ula, my dog
U tterly unusual
L azy Labrador
A dorable animal.

Kristen Hughes (9)
West Park CE Middle School, Worthing

Shih-Tzu

She walks in beauty like an angel wobbling
Up and down all around in her first walk
A little bowl nearly the size of her
As she touches her first ball
Then at night she sleeps in beauty.

As she wanders slowly around
Up and down all around
She finally finds her way
Whining for her first walk.

And then one day she escaped
Looking for another dog
Then she finds her way home
In the silent night
Then she finds her pups!

Emily Scott (9)
West Park CE Middle School, Worthing

Love Is A Funny Feeling

Love is a funny feeling
The symbol is hearts
The day is Valentine's Day
When you buy cards and chocs.

It involves hugs and kisses
You go to theme parks
Or you can go to the park
It can be happy and upsetting.

To love you have to trust your partner
And understand when you break up
It breaks your heart
You realise you can never be apart.

Eleanor Leach (10)
West Park CE Middle School, Worthing

I Love To Dance

I n position my feet ready to go, my body is swaying to and fro
The music fills the air like the scent of a flower as my body builds up its power

L unging, leaping high and low, twisting, turning shapes as I go
O utstretched arms and pointed toes
My body is swaying to and fro
V anishing into another world, the music carries me up and beyond
E ffortlessly moving myself around the room, I'm flying high in the sky like a bird

T he music makes me want to perform, silk sequins,
the whole shebang
O pera, jazz, I don't mind, my body is swaying to and fro

D ancing is my passion, it's all I want to do
A nything else really won't do
N ever give up, that's the way, practice makes perfect in every way
C horeography helps the dance come to life
E ndless energy I have when I dance.

Amy Goacher (10)
West Park CE Middle School, Worthing

I Love Dogs

Dogs are dogs, they can be nothing more and nothing less
Dogs can do competitions, dogs can be working dogs
Dogs can just be pets
Dogs are dogs, they can be nothing more and nothing less
Dogs can do agility, dogs can run, jump and hide
Dogs are dogs, they can be nothing more and nothing less
Dogs are just dogs!

Kate Davies (9)
West Park CE Middle School, Worthing

My School Day

When walking to school, I always say,
'Why does it have to be this way?'
I see the gates draw near
Turn to Mum and shed a tear
Overflow with sadness when I hear
Mum saying, 'Goodbye,' so close, so near.

Walk to the playground, sniff the air
Taste the cool wind, smell bacon from somewhere
Hear my friends chatting, leap for joy
Can't wait to show off my new toy.

Enter the classroom, feeling fresh
Hear the register, today's the test!
Go to the whiteboard, feel its smooth surface
Return to my seat, finger my lace.

Revise for my exam, take comfort in my book
Bite my lip, will I remember? Take another look
Smell fresh ink, hear the scratch of pens
Breathe in deep and count to ten.

Nervousness reverberates, absolute silence, I mustn't forget
I lick my lips, taste salty sweat
The new paper emits an inviting smell
I look at it desperately, will I do well?

Later, at lunch, the nightmare's over now
My friends crowd round me asking, 'How did you do? How?'
Overcome with relief, I can't speak a word
Nibble my lunch distractedly like a bird
Everyone relaxing at last, eating together is nice
In my opinion, it's paradise!

Kathryn Reynolds (9)
West Park CE Middle School, Worthing

Animals Are So Cool

Frogs, frogs are so cool
They can jump higher than you.

Dogs, dogs are so cool
They can dig better than you.

Cats, cats are so cool
They can run faster than you.

Spiders, spiders are so cool
They have hairier legs than you.

Snakes, snakes are so cool
They can slide better than you.

Freja Coombes (10)
West Park CE Middle School, Worthing

Hungry

My dad has an eating problem
He is very overweight
Chocolate, doughnuts and pizza too
And chips upon his plate.

Daddy's trying to thin down a bit
He started jogging to keep fit
Also hoping to have some fun
But stepped on the scales and weighed a ton.

Mum was being very harsh
Making him eat cucumber and grass
So Daddy sneaked to the corner shop
And bought himself a bottle of pop.

Cameron Huggins (10)
West Park CE Middle School, Worthing

Robots

As the speeders zoomed towards the enemy,
The fighter jets flew overhead,
Meanwhile the robots charged,
Towards the well-defended forts,
At the back of this mighty army
The commander planned his fierce attack.

As this great army reached the fort,
The speeders mounted a counter-attack
The robots started to open fire,
With lasers all ablaze,
But the humans had proved more powerful,
Than the robots ever thought.

Yet, unbeknown to the humans,
The fighter jets were ready to attack
With guns ablazing, the jets swooped down,
Taking the humans by surprise
The robots outnumbered the humans
As they blasted through the fort gates.

The humans fled to many places,
Many surrendered to the robots,
The fort fell to the amazing army,
Who rebuilt it for further defence,
Robots were rapidly taking over humankind
And the human world.

Jacob Pennels (9)
West Park CE Middle School, Worthing

The Four Seasons

Hear the birds fluttering in the breeze
And the rustle of the trees
See the leaves falling, one by one
Oh, one just tickled my thumb
This is spring, here comes summer
It's going to be much funnier!

The clouds up high in the sky
And the plants, look like they could dance
Here is summer, next comes autumn
It's going to be great!

See the sun shining on my iced bun
Also, the grass as shiny as brass
It's autumn, nearly winter
Ow, I've got a splinter.

Here comes the snow which looks like dough
I am really cold, soon I would mould
Here is winter, we're at the end of the year
Let's put our feet up and have a beer!

Matthew Lay (10)
West Park CE Middle School, Worthing

Young Writers Information

We hope you have enjoyed reading this book - and that you will continue to enjoy it in the coming years.

If you like reading and writing poetry drop us a line, or give us a call, and we'll send you a free information pack.

Alternatively if you would like to order further copies of this book or any of our other titles, then please give us a call or log onto our website at www.youngwriters.co.uk

Young Writers Information
Remus House
Coltsfoot Drive
Peterborough
PE2 9JX

(01733) 890066